Children's Understanding of Disability

This book is a valuable addition to the debate surrounding the integration of children with special needs into ordinary schools. Taking the viewpoint of the children themselves, it looks at how pupils with severe learning difficulties and their non-disabled class mates interact.

Ann Lewis examines what happened when non-disabled pupils and pupils with severe learning difficulties worked together regularly over the course of a year. The book explores, from the perspectives of both groups, their preparation for collaborative activities, their attitudes and understanding and the characteristics of their communication. It contains analyses of what non-disabled children understood about the nature of learning difficulties, how non-disabled pupils tutored pupils with learning difficulties and how, in turn, those pupils asserted themselves. In addition, Ann Lewis includes the views of children working in segregated special education. Throughout, the emphasis is on pupils' views and the possible reasons for their opinions and actions.

Ann Lewis is a Senior Lecturer in Education at the University of Warwick and her publications include *Primary Special Needs and the National Curriculum* (Routledge 1991).

Children's Understanding of Disability

Ann Lewis

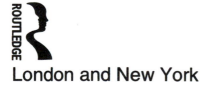

London and New York

First published 1995
by Routledge
11 New Fetter Lane, London EC4P 4EE

Simultaneously published in the USA and Canada
by Routledge
29 West 35th Street, New York, NY 10001

Typeset in Palatino by
Michael Mepham, Frome, Somerset

Printed and bound in Great Britain by
Mackays of Chatham PLC, Chatham, Kent

British Library Cataloguing in Publication Data
A catalogue record for this book is available from the
British Library

Library of Congress Cataloguing in Publication Data
A catalogue record for this book has been requested

ISBN 0–415–10131–X (hbk)
ISBN 0–415–10132–8 (pbk)

Contents

Figures

Acknowledgements

My thanks to the anonymised pupils, staff and parents involved in these projects. Their enthusiasm, convictions, openness about both successes and limitations, and a willingness to share their experiences, have enabled the conclusions to be presented more widely. I hope that the children who allowed their pictures to be presented here (in the text and on the cover) will be pleased with the results.

Many colleagues and 'critical friends' have shaped the process of reflecting on and analysing the events depicted here. In particular my thanks to Barry Carpenter, Mo Daniels, Jeremy Fathers, Frances Gardner, Mal Leicester, Mel Lloyd-Smith, Pam Maras, Julie Moore, Arlene Ramasut and Anne Sinclair-Taylor for their supportive and incisive comments on earlier drafts. I am grateful to Gordon Elias and Pat Long for advice concerning terms used outside the UK.

Helen Fairlie at Routledge has been instrumental in translating the idea into the book and her continuing support is warmly appreciated.

My special thanks to Gerry for reading countless drafts and again tolerating the associated domestic disruption and frenzy.

Part of Chapter 5 has appeared in the *British Journal of Special Education* (1994, vol. 21, no. 3, pp. 101–4) and is reproduced with permission.

Glossary

severe learning difficulties (UK) are approximately comparable
with:
   moderate intellectual disabilities (Australia / New Zealand)
   moderate to severe mental retardation or trainable mentally
      retarded (USA / Canada)

moderate learning difficulties (UK) are approximately comparable
with:
   moderate to mild intellectual disability (Australia / New
      Zealand)
   mild mental retardation or educable mentally retarded
      (USA / Canada)

Note: See pages 8–10.

Transcription conventions

(..)	pause (number of dots indicative of approximate length in seconds)
?	rising inflection
!	animated inflection
WOW	italics denote emphasis
WOW	upper case denotes volume
WOW	bold type denotes very loud volume
(( ))	information about actions (in parentheses)
((?))	doubt concerning information about actions
( )	no response or vocalisation not interpretable
[ ]	comment on interaction (in square brackets)
[?]	doubt about comment on interaction
(hey?)	doubt about transcription

Chapter 1

Setting the scene

When I was 15 I spent a summer working at a children's camp run and organised by a national charity. The camp was unusual, not least because, although it was held in one of England's leading public schools, it was not for pupils from that school. The children who joined the camp made an unusual mix. Half were deemed to be 'at risk' due to the high level of poverty in their East London homes. They were surprised, if not overawed, by the school with its wood-panelled rooms, oil paintings and half-hidden trunks of exotic clothes. The London children were initially bemused by the other group of children who came to the camp. This latter group all had severe physical disabilities. They tended to arrive with cases full of medical paraphernalia and letters specifying what they should not, for health reasons, be allowed to do.

When these disparate children arrived I could not imagine how the camp could possibly work successfully. On the second day, Meghan (a 10 year old with hydrocephalus) and Danny (an 8-year-old Londoner) had disappeared after breakfast. As I was supposed to be in charge of these children I was worried about them and embarrassed at this early indication of my ineptitude. I visualised Meghan hiding somewhere in the building and close to death while Danny was hitch-hiking back to London. However, eventually I found the children – both sitting in a large bath, with sponges and scouring powder in their hands, cleaning the bath. Meghan had decided that, as she was never allowed to do anything like that at home, she was determined to get into the bath and clean it. Danny had some idea of what to do, had taken a liking to Meghan, and offered to show her how to clean the sides of the bath. Perhaps they recognised in one another their shared qualities – tenacity, a sense of humour and determined independence. They remained good friends all week and were a constant reminder that I had initially seen, not individuals, but a personification of the labels 'poverty' and 'disability'.

The experience showed me that children are often limited more by others' expectations and consequent labelling than by intrinsic 'conditions'. My subsequent involvement in moves towards developing inclusive schools has reinforced this message. I do not know how Danny and Meghan felt about others' expectations of them. However, what it felt like to be on the receiving end of low expectations has been recalled powerfully by Michelle Thomas:

> When I was in school they wouldn't teach you to write as a letter, they would call letters objects – like they used to call the letter H a chair and they used to say the letter M was a mountain. It was a boarding school – a special school – I went there from when I was 6 to when I was 9. I couldn't read by then and they said I was unteachable. I was always ill at school and slow at learning things. They said I was unteachable, that I couldn't be taught anything. That's why I had to leave. They hadn't taught me things, only these things – H is a chair, M is a mountain. When I left I was only tiny and I was sorry because I'd made some friends there. I was confused because I didn't know why I was leaving, I didn't understand that I hadn't learned anything. I left school on the Friday and I thought, 'Oh, I'll be back on Sunday' but I didn't go back . . . I didn't understand until my mother said, 'You've left school, they've taken you out of school, they said you were unteachable'.
>
> (1990: 33)

An alternative view, highlighting the impact of positive expectations, is described by Donna Williams in her autobiography. She comments that the only thing she missed in her schooling was 'inclusion', by which she means acceptance by other children and teachers. One high point for her was a particular teacher:

> Mr Reynolds never emphasised disability, but instead allowed me to show him what I was capable of, and he would tell me things which I did better than the others . . . His mood never changed. He never seemed to betray my trust.
>
> (1992: 42)

ETHOS

This book explores what happened when children and young people from special schools (for pupils with severe learning difficulties) and mainstream schools worked together regularly over a series of school years in an attempt to develop integrated classes. Doing this meant changing both sets of schools. In this process the schools set out to learn from, and through, collaboration with one another. Many, although not all, of the staff in the schools shared a belief that ultimately, and with the necessary resources, many pupils from special schools could and should be educated effectively alongside mainstream school peers. They believed that this would be to the benefit of both special and mainstream school pupils. This reflected a wider underlying belief that disabled people should be included as fully as possible in their local communities.

Tackling this broader issue raises questions about care in the community, the role of advertising in promoting images of unrealisable physical perfection at one end of the scale and helpless invalidism at the other, and the roles and portrayal of charities. These are beyond the scope of this book but all relate to the polarisation of disabled and non-disabled people.

This polarisation masks four things which have relevance for integration at school level. These are, first, a merging, in reality, of disabled and non-disabled categories. We are all, to some extent and in some ways, disabled. Recognising this is a deterrent to condemning the disabled as abnormal and treating the minor imperfections of us all as faults to be denied or disguised. Some commentators acknowledge the converse of this by referring to the 'differently gifted' or 'differently abled'.

Second, disabled people are as diverse as the rest of the population and grouping them under disability labels encourages a false homogeneity in perceptions of those people. This needs to be borne in mind when reference is made later to pupils at particular types of special schools.

Third, presenting the disabled as a discrete and relatively dependent group obscures our common interdependence.

Fourth, while physical or mental perfection and individual autonomy are valued above imperfection and dependence, the members of society who are seen as reflecting the latter qualities will remain pitied or patronised.

Integration

In the literature there has been increasing dissatisfaction with the term 'integration' because it has often been used or interpreted in a narrow sense of placement only. Children moved from any special to any mainstream school context may be said to be 'integrated'. Yet this says nothing about the quality of that integration. What one person describes as integration may be seen by another person as segregation in a new form. The American term 'maindumping', to describe a child with disabilities or learning difficulties who is placed in an unready or unwilling mainstream school, conveys this ambiguity. Placement in a mainstream school is a necessary, but not a sufficient, condition for realising the goals of integration. Integration as placement also overlooks the process of moving from a segregated to an integrated system.

Sue Szivos has made a critique of the literature on normalisation (much of which has influenced moves towards educational integration) from a social psychological perspective. She notes,

> Herein lies one of the central contradictions of normalisation in that while it purports to revalue people with disabilities, it is rooted in a hostility to, and denial of 'differentness' . . . We should also ask whether in denying labels we are also denying and devaluing difference.
>
> (1992: 126–7)

Sue Szivos also draws attention to the assumption that to be attributed value, disadvantaged groups should aspire to fulfil society's idealised norms. The conclusion of her critique is not that we should abandon attempts at integration but that we need to recognise the complexities underlying the process.

Inclusion

As a result of such concerns about the term 'integration', the word 'inclusion' has come to be used to convey both placement and certain qualities of that placement. 'Inclusion' emphasises that what is being described is something that is neither special nor mainstream school but a new amalgam. The difficulty in operationalising such an ideal is illustrated in evaluations of the Australian experiences of moves towards inclusion in Victoria (Mousley *et al.*, 1993). These researchers noted, 'Ideas arising from the practices of "special" education are being imposed on the integration process, limiting teachers' visions of educational opportunity for all . . .. Teachers are regarding integration as being yet another form of specialism' (1993: 59, 68).

The term inclusion draws attention to the quality of the mainstream school context as a whole and for all children, not just the disabled. Inclusion is described variously as:

Being with one another . . . how we deal with diversity, how we deal with difference

(Forest and Pearpoint, 1992)

The presence of all learners in one shared educational community

(Hall, 1992)

A set of principles which ensures that the student with a disability is viewed as a valued and needed member of the school community in every respect

(Uditsky, 1993)

These descriptions highlight different emphases in the way in which 'inclusion' is used. It may stress attitudes being promoted (notably an acceptance of human diversity and a respect for individuals) and/or to the location of pupils (i.e. in a common institution). Thus inclusion is both a means (a particular ethos) and an end (non-segregated schools). One may have reservations about inclusion as necessarily all-inclusive but still support the ethos being promoted. In theory, an acceptance of diversity could be promoted through segregated systems. For example, it is reported that in the Netherlands a highly differentiated, and growing, special school system is not associated with negative stereotyping of pupils in special education but is seen as a valued specialist resource (Meijer *et al.*, 1994).

The rhetoric of inclusion obscures what is being underemphasised or ignored and leaves underlying value judgements unexamined. In the US context, inclusive schools have been described by some academics as defying straightforward interpretation and they have written of the increasing stridency and insularity about inclusive schools (Fuchs and Fuchs, 1994). The descriptions given earlier do not refer to two major themes in current educational discourse – parental choice and educational priorities. These are, implicitly, seen as being of secondary importance to the promotion of certain attitudes. Whether one agrees with this is a matter of individual value judgements and will reflect in part beliefs about the extent to which education should be a vehicle for changing society.

Parents and/or pupils may choose or wish for a segregated school. Rightly or wrongly, a totally inclusive system removes this choice. Equally, if inclusive schools are not available then parents do not have the chance to exercise this choice.

Parents and/or pupils may also have different priorities from those advocated by individuals arguing for inclusive schools. For example, the attainment of certain self-help or communication skills may be seen as of over-riding importance by some parents and therefore the preferred educational environment will be the one that best fosters these skills. Two extreme examples of this are given by Robert Henderson (1993) reviewing integration policy in the USA. He reported that alongside some strong parental movements for inclusion, some parents have insisted that their children attend residential special schools. This has happened even when the local school has what it believes to be an appropriate programme for the child. Two major parent groups have been involved: parents of adolescents with severe emotional problems and parents with severe hearing loss whose children also have severe hearing impairments. Some educationalists have argued similarly that education encompasses, rather than contrasts with, care and that curricular entitlement should not deny within-child factors (Jordan and Powell, 1994). From this perspective, a special school may be preferred over a mainstream placement.

A number of writers have made links between the processes involved in developing inclusive schools and the characteristics of effective schools (see Fulcher, 1989; Slee, 1993; Ramasut and Reynolds, 1993). The approach is summarised in Mel Ainscow's words: 'I am proposing . . . that the special needs task is reconstructed as a process of school improvement' (1993: 8). However, overall structures and processes in schools mask variability in individual experiences. As Seamus Hegarty (1993) has pointed out, the effective school is an abstraction and outlines what works for most pupils for most of the time in relation to certain, often narrowly defined, criteria. Moves towards developing inclusive schools need to be examined in terms of the multi-faceted impact on individuals, especially all the pupils in whose interests, ostensibly, the changes have been made.

The term 'integration' is used in this book when placement is being emphasised; 'inclusion' is used when a school ethos that explictly aims to respond to pupils' diversity is being emphasised.

Normality

Interpretations of children's behaviour are often referenced to what is deemed to constitute 'normal' development. There are two inherent problems in this. First, it underemphasises the variability encompassed by what is 'normal'; second, normality is assumed to be what typifies the majority – that is, what is usual. Each of these will be considered in more detail.

It is difficult to shift from a normative framework into a conceptual framework that conceives development as varied, encompassing diverse patterns. Developmental scales such as those of Mary Sheridan (1973) and similar checklists distributed at many post-natal clinics identify clear expectations about normality. Some developmental scales provide slightly broader bands but retain the emphasis on 'normal' targets (for example, Denver Developmental Charts, Frankenberg, 1981). For example, children are expected to be able to scribble at 2 years and to thread beads at 3 years. This immediately places children who do not scribble and thread at these times as 'abnormal'. Earlier than this may be regarded as evidence of high ability. Conversely, later than this (or not at all) identifies the child, by implication, as slow. Such a view is entrenched and anomalies such as late developers who are also very gifted (for example, Leonardo da Vinci) tend to be seen as bizarre exceptions rather than as an indication that normality may have been conceived too narrowly.

The possible inappropriateness for the majority of what is deemed to be normal is illustrated by the QWERTY keyboard that is used for nearly all typewriter and word processor keyboards. It is, in practice, very inefficient for most people who are not touch typists. Most users of these keyboards are 'hunt and peck' typists using two fingers. The development of keyboards for disabled people may well turn out to have considerable benefits for the majority. 'Normality', in this example, reflects only an atypical minority.

In addition to these conceptual problems, value judgements

associated with 'normality' tend to place it as superior to abnor-
mality. This is curious given the opposite situation in other
contexts. For example, rare birds are rated more highly by bird-
watchers than are common species, limited editions of a design
raise more money at auction than do more usual versions, and a
postage stamp with a fault is a treasured find. Jenny Corbett has
written a refreshingly vigorous attack on 'normality' and concluded, 'I, for one, would feel most insulted if I was ever labelled
"normal". It seems to embody confinement and restraint; a
pinched, arid meanness' (1991: 260).

Impairment, disability and handicap

Impairment, disability and handicap are commonly used and related terms. David Thomas (1978) elaborated the distinctions
between them. *Impairment* is a neutral term to mean the loss of
structure or function (such as hearing loss). *Disability* is the impact
of the impairment (for example, poor speech may be the result of
a hearing loss). *Handicap* is the impact of the impairment or disability as a result of others' negative evaluation of it (for example,
poor speech becomes a handicap if it causes others to be patronising). Disability and handicap have different connotations
although my computer-based grammar-check program tells me
that I should replace 'handicap' with 'disability'!

Learning difficulties

There has been extensive debate internationally about the definitions of learning difficulties and learning disabilities (see, for
example, Franklin, 1987; Norwich, 1990; Wang *et al.*, 1990). The
purpose here is not to debate these definitions but, for readers who
are unfamiliar with the UK education system, to give an indication
of the groups being described in this research.

The 1978 Warnock Report on Special Educational Needs (DES,
1978) in the UK recommended that the term learning difficulties be
used to describe a very broad group of children exhibiting difficulties in learning. The Report recommended four sub-divisions: mild,
moderate, severe and specific. This book concerns two sub-groups
of children with learning difficulties: those with severe learning
difficulties (SLD) and those with moderate learning difficulties
(MLD).

Children with SLD form an heterogeneous group (Mittler, 1992; Tilstone, 1992a). In the UK, prior to the Warnock Report, these children were referred to as being mentally handicapped or as severely educationally sub-normal. Many of these pupils have specific language difficulties in addition to more general cognitive or sensory impairments. These difficulties may be primarily with interpreting language or with expression, that is communicating a message, or with both sending and receiving messages. However, some pupils with SLD have no additional language problems. Initial causes of SLD are predominantly medical. Within the SLD population some children have multiple and profound handicaps. The SLD school pupils in the studies reported here did not have profound and multiple learning difficulties.

The comparable group in the USA are children who are re-garded as moderately to severely mentally retarded or trainable mentally retarded. Mental retardation is defined by the American Association on Mental Retardation as 'significantly subaverage general intellectual functioning existing concurrently with deficits in adaptive behavior and manifested during the developmental period' (Grossman, 1983, cited in Kirk *et al.*, 1993). Some writers have sub-divided levels of mental retardation according to broad IQ bands with IQs of under 35 representing severe and profound mental retardation, IQs of 35–55 (approximately) representing moderate mental retardation and IQs of 50–70 (approximately) representing mild mental retardation (Kirk *et al.*, 1993). In Australia and New Zealand an approximately comparable group to the children described in the UK as having severe learning difficulties are children with moderate intellectual disabilities.

Children with moderate learning difficulties (MLD) are an equally heterogenous group and even more difficult to define. Initial causes for their learning difficulties may be a combination of medical, sensory, environmental and behavioural factors. The poorer social groups are over-represented in the MLD school popu-lation. In the UK, children regarded as having MLD may attend special (MLD) schools or they may be in mainstream schools, usually with additional support.

Groups in other countries which are broadly comparable with the MLD group in the UK are children with mild mental retarda-tion (USA) or children with mild to moderate intellectual disabilities (Australia/New Zealand).

Discussion about pupils with learning difficulties and cross-cultural comparisons are complicated by this diversity as well as by the use of different definitions for the group studied and the hazy relationship between disability and educational provision. Definitions of, and terms to encompass, learning difficulty vary between countries and, when in different languages, may be distorted in translation. It is not clear whether, for example, children designated 'trainable mentally retarded' (USA), having moderate intellectual disabilities (Australia and New Zealand) or severe learning difficulties (UK) represent similar groups. In addition, there is often variation within countries, by region and by service, in the definition and description of comparable groups. For example, in the UK, Education Departments refer to people with learning difficulties while an overlapping group is referred to by Social Services as having learning disabilities. Similarly, Margaret Wang and her co-authors (1990) have discussed the wide variation in classification criteria and procedures across states and local school districts within the USA.

There is no straightforward relationship between disability label and educational provision. So the source of the research sample involving children with learning difficulties may bias results. For example, if the sample is drawn from special schools then it will be affected by the intake policy of the school or area. In the UK, children with similar types of learning difficulty might attend a mainstream school, a school for pupils with moderate learning difficulties or a school for pupils with severe learning difficulties. The school attended will depend on local policy and on parental preferences.

THE INTERNATIONAL CONTEXT

In 1981 UNICEF estimated that of the 140 million disabled children in the world, 63 per cent lived in Asia, 13 per cent in Africa and 9 per cent in Latin America. Globally, Europe, North America and Australasia accounted for only a small minority of the world's disabled children. In about one-third of the world, disabled children were excluded from the formal school system (Mittler, 1990).

Integration is increasingly being seen as a 'rights' issue (Roaf and Bines, 1989; Leicester, 1992; Lewis, 1993a). Under the United Nations Convention (1992) disabled children have a right to be helped to achieve the greatest possible degree of self-reliance and social integration. The United Nations declaration does not come down unequivocally on the side of either integrated or segregated provision, rather it emphasises the child's right to provision which will develop all his or her capabilities to the fullest extent. Overall, where disabled children do receive an education, there has been a trend towards integration. A worldwide survey of children with special needs in mainstream schools was carried out by OMEP, the European pre-school organisation, in 1991. Seventeen of the twenty-one countries surveyed (from Europe, Asia, the Americas, and Australasia) had recently passed pro-integration legislation. Legislation in Sweden, Australia, Canada, Italy, the UK, Spain, the USA and elsewhere signals widespread support for schools that operate integration policies. Elsewhere such moves have been noted as ultimate goals by countries such as Pakistan and Ireland, in which largely segregated systems are still operating (see further reading).

Attitudes towards inclusive education do not operate in isolation from broader attitudes in society. Ralf Georg Reuth, in his (1993) biography of Joseph Goebbels, reports that Goebbels was 4 years old when he contracted osteomyelitis. This left him with a club foot. His family, devout Catholics, interpreted this as a curse from God. More recently, Robert Heath and Paula Levin (1991) describe work showing that in China, blindness is taken to signify that something is wrong in the family; while in Hispanic families a disabled child is regarded as a test of religious conviction – a metaphorical cross for the family to bear. Culturally based attitudes are surely bound to influence children's and teachers' attitudes to disability. Will the Chinese stance discourage integration? Will the Hispanic view encourage integration but also foster low expectations of disabled children?

Some regions have provided powerful demonstrations of what can be achieved when there is the political, professional and parental will to develop inclusive education (see further reading on the comparative dimension to integration). In Massachusetts (USA), Connecticut (USA), Ontario (Canada), Victoria (Australia), Spain, Italy, Derbyshire (England) and Cardiff (Wales), among other places, alliances of parents, pupils and professionals have formed to argue for wider and more effective integration. The voices of disabled people, released through burgeoning self-advocacy movements, have sharpened the sense of urgency about the importance of inclusion.

Alongside these movements there have also been reservations

expressed about integration, both as a principle and, more commonly, in terms of its outcomes in practice (discussed by Hornby, 1992, *re* the UK, Mousley *et al.*, 1993, *re* Australia, and Fuchs and Fuchs, 1994, *re* the USA). If integration is regarded as not working, this may be due to a wide range of factors. Criticism of the practice does not necessarily imply rejection of the principle. Reservations about the practice of integration have focused on finance / resource issues, the increasing bureaucratisation of integration (and associated labelling of some children) and claimed superficiality of contact.

Reservations about the practice of integration have included claims that it has been merely a smokescreen in order to make savings in education budgets. Max Hunt has reviewed integration policy and practice in one area of the UK and concluded that 'appropriately resourced integration is likely to be more expensive than a reasonably efficient special school' (1994: 4). Whether this is the case will presumably depend to a large extent on how adequately integrated schools are resourced. Some savings are likely to be made through, for example, reduced transport costs but if there is a commitment to integration then mainstream schools will also need more specialist resources and expertise. Findings from case studies of the integration of pupils with sensory impairments in five regions in the UK supported the view that integration is not a cheap option (Coopers and Lybrand, 1992). There were few additional staffing costs overall but high initial sums were needed for providing both appropriate resources and general staff training to mainstream schools.

The increasing bureacracy associated with integration and the dangers of labelling 'the integration child' have been noted in many countries. This has led John Lewis, writing about the Australian context, to conclude, 'The future of integration in Victoria schools is problematic' (1993: 23).

There have been reports of reservations about the outcomes of integrated education in Sweden and the USA, both of which were early proponents of integration (see further reading). In Sweden, for example, it is reported that integration has often been at a social, rather than curricular, level for some children. The pupils may play together but they are not tackling the same curriculum, differentiated for individual needs. In both Sweden and the USA concerns have been expressed about the viability of integrating children with severe disabilities into mainstream schools.

Interestingly, a number of cross-cultural comparisons have reached common conclusions. James Ward and his co-workers have carried out extensive research into integration in New South Wales and made comparisons with other Australian, Canadian and UK contexts. They predicted that although there were many problems in implementing integration policies, the obstacles were likely to be overcome as education systems develop which combine social justice with effective instruction for children with disabilities or learning difficulties (Ward *et al.*, 1994). Finally, in an extensive review of integration in six countries Jan Rispens (1994) concluded that although much progress has been made towards integration, there are still many problems to be solved. He called for a better understanding of the practical difficulties involved in implementing integration.

LINK PROJECTS

The link projects described in the later chapters involved part-time placement (for example, for half a day a week) during which groups of special school pupils attended mainstream schools, or vice versa. During these sessions the mainstream and special school pupils worked together on tasks that required each pupil to participate in the shared activity.

The scene below is typical of thousands of similar scenes, captured on video or audio tape, and recorded during link sessions:

> Robert, age 11, is smiling broadly. Next to him sits Natalie, 14 years old. She is staring intently at Robert trying to work out what he is saying. They have been working together for almost an hour and concentration has rarely lapsed for either pupil. Now they have nearly finished their task. The product of this long bout of serious concentration is half a page of writing about their favourite things. The television soap *Neighbours* and biscuits are shared favourites. They have different favourite teachers. Robert attends a mainstream primary school; Natalie attends a nearby school for pupils with severe learning difficulties.

What do these children feel about their work partners? Does Robert understand why Natalie sometimes behaves in unusual ways? Does Natalie understand that Robert is often afraid of going to school and feels he is bottom of the class in a high pressure, high achieving middle class school? How do Natalie and Robert get through the complicated business of communicating with one another so successfully? These questions are addresssed in the following chapters.

Link projects have been termed 'peripheral schemes', 'partial integration' and 'incremental integration'. The term used reflects, to some extent, the degree of support for the approach. Despite reservations by some commentators link projects have been, and continue to be, developed in many countries. A survey by the National Foundation for Educational Research (NFER) in England and Wales, in 1985, found that half the 268 special schools surveyed had pupils going to mainstream schools on a regular basis (Jowett *et al.*, 1988). A parallel survey nine years later, and five years after the introduction of the UK National Curriculum in 1989, found that this had increased. Seventy per cent of the 898 special schools surveyed then had pupils going to mainstream schools at least once a week (Fletcher-Campbell, 1994). These visits tended to be for a short period of time (under half a day per week) and for a small number of pupils.

Link schemes involving pupils moving between special and mainstream schools are seen by their supporters as a justifiable end in themselves and/or as a step towards fuller integration and inclusion. Some potential strengths of such link schemes (in addition to, potentially, more general benefits of integration) are:

- the use of both special and mainstream school expertise,
- enhanced opportunities for interaction for both groups of pupils,
- a lack of disruption to other curricular arrangements,
- a trial period for fuller integration,
- the provision of opportunities for in-service work with staff involved at both schools,
- the transfer of special school skills to mainstream school settings,
- the transfer of mainstream school skills to special school settings,
- continuity across a series of link schemes, which may enable pupils to sustain friendships over a long period despite class, and even school, transfers,
- a supportive introduction to integration for parents, school governors and support staff,

- a supported re-introduction to mainstream schooling for many children who have, by definition, been failed by or failed in mainstream schooling once already, and
- a sustaining of specialised resources.

Against these strengths, there are possible disadvantages. Such link schemes may:

- not challenge either school to change practice and become more inclusive,
- always see the visiting set of pupils as visitors rather than classmates,
- produce difficulties over resources and transport costs,
- be for schools so far apart that much time is spent in travelling,
- have visiting pupils from a different local commmunity and so pupils will not meet outside the link sessions,
- be too brief and/or fragmentary to allow friendships to be built up,
- involve large groups of children descending on the other school, and
- be vulnerable to external constraints such as other demands on the time.

The accounts in this book provide a fine-grained look at what occurred in such link schemes. The large numbers of pupils making the links are probably unusual. However, the evidence should help to evaluate the strengths and limitations of link projects, to find ways of maximising the strengths while limiting the disadvantages, and to review what place such link schemes may have in promoting an inclusive ethos in mainstream schools.

STRUCTURE OF THE BOOK

I have deliberately chosen to concentrate on the views and experiences of the pupils involved in link schemes. What adults do and say is important but that would take another book and there are texts that cover that ground in other contexts (for example, Bennett and Cass, 1989; Booth and Potts, 1983; Hegarty et al., 1981, 1982; Bell and Colbeck, 1989; Jowett et al., 1988).

Chapter 2 looks at what children in segregated special education felt about schools and teachers. Some key themes here are feelings about friends, teachers and control. The discussion is based on findings from interviews with nearly sixty children attending two schools for pupils with moderate learning difficulties (MLD). These children's responses relate to their perceptions, that is the meanings they have attached to special and mainstream school experiences. Their accounts show what they valued in school and hence what is likely to be particularly important for them in an inclusive school.

The structure of the book then follows, broadly, the life in one year of each of the two link schemes. Both of these were initiated and run by the schools involved. One of these projects involved ten 6 to 7 year olds from a mainstream school working with ten 4 to 8 year olds from a school for pupils with severe learning difficulties (SLD). The children met in fortnightly half-day sessions. These were planned alternately by special and mainstream school staff and were held in the mainstream school. Most of the mainstream school children involved were 7 years old so this project is referred to as the Link 7 project.

The other project involved three groups of eleven 10 to 11 year olds from a mainstream school working with nine 12 to 15 year olds from a school for pupils with SLD. This work is referred to as the Link 11 project. These pupils met for weekly half-day sessions over one school year. The sessions were held in the special school and, as in the Link 7 project, were planned alternately by special and mainstream school staff.

There were three main sources of information about pupils' interactions in, and reactions to, the link projects. First, special and mainstream school pupils working together were audio or video recorded throughout two school years (one year for each project). From this there were, in total, nearly 3000 recorded minutes of observations during which special and mainstream school pupils worked on a shared task. Second, all the mainstream school pupils involved in the two link projects were interviewed. The views of pupils from the special schools were collected directly through informal conversations with them and indirectly through their teachers' reflections. Third, a cross-section of teachers involved in the link projects kept diaries in which they recorded their plans, expectations and reactions to events in the sessions.

The evidence presented is inevitably partial. It does not tell us about the link scheme pupils' experiences in segregated settings or about wider aspects of the integrated context, such as teacher attitudes or resources. However, it does provide what has previously not been analysed and discussed, that is detailed evidence about the responses of a range of individual pupils (from special and mainstream schools) to the integrated setting.

Chapter 3 examines the groundwork for these projects: the aims behind them, how parents reacted and what a typical session was like. It looks at how the pupils were introduced, the importance of structure, some of the apprehensions expressed by the adults involved and, more broadly, the implications for fostering an inclusive ethos. A wide range of published materials and approaches from other sources that could be used to foster such a climate are summarised.

Chapters 4 and 5 discuss ways in which the pupils interacted once they had got to know one another. These interactions happened to take place in a school but they are of wider relevance. They have implications for relationships in families that include children with disabilities or difficulties, as well as for other social settings. Chapter 4 focuses on the Link 7 project, particularly the children from the mainstream school. Chapter 5 focuses on the Link 11 project through the eyes of four of the special school pupils.

Chapter 6 looks at the end of the year of link sessions and the perceptions of the pupils involved. This chapter draws out, in particular, the confusions and complexities arising from misunderstandings of the mainstream school children about the nature of severe learning difficulties. Changes in understanding at ages 7 and 11 are related to broad developmental changes in conceptual thinking.

Finally Chapter 7 examines seven overarching themes emerging from the studies. These themes include the impact of 'visitor' status on interaction, the drive to communicate generated in the link sessions and adults' roles in dealing with 'misbehaviour'.

Chapter 2

Views of children in segregated special education

The focus of this book is on the views and interactions of children and young people involved in link projects. This chapter provides a wider context through discussion of the views of children in segregated special education.

There have been moves in many countries towards greater integration (summarised in Chapter 1). What do pupils with special needs feel about this? This chapter looks at what some children attending special schools for pupils with moderate learning difficulties (MLD) recalled about mainstream and special schools. The emerging themes relate to how pupils felt about being powerful (or powerless) and a sense of self-worth. The chapter is organised under the key topics of school transfer, teachers and discipline, playtime (recess/break), friends and the curriculum.

COLLECTING PRIMARY AGE CHILDREN'S VIEWS OF SCHOOLING

In the 1960s, studies of the views about school of children attending mainstream schools generally involved pupils of secondary school age. Possibly, younger children were thought to be too unreliable to make it worth taking their views seriously. However, later studies showed that primary age children were also able to make perceptive and pertinent observations about their teachers and schooling.

Children and adults may have different ideas about what is the most appropriate educational provision for the child. There are many anecdotal reports about parents wishing for segregated provision while the child wants integrated provision, or vice versa. For example, some parents may be enthusiastic about their child having extra tuition within the mainstream school (for example, in reading) but to the child this may require an unwelcome separation from classmates. Alternatively, the child might want to go to a special school because of unusual resources there. These may include, for example, soft play areas or extra information technology equipment. However, the child's parents may feel that this would make the child less familiar to other children in the home neighbourhood and so make the child relatively isolated in the community.

In general, children at mainstream primary schools seem to be satisfied and happy at school (see further reading on children's views of schooling). We know less about what children in segregated special education feel about school. Barrie Wade and Maggie Moore (1992) investigated the views of a wide range of pupils with special educational needs (in the UK, Australia and New Zealand). They found that most pupils were positive about their teachers and lessons. At primary level, children in segregated settings were slightly more positive about enjoying lessons than were children in integrated settings. About three-quarters of these children described their teachers as helpful; there was little difference between pupils in segregated or integrated settings.

We need to be careful about reading too much into these findings. Pupils may have been isolated and worked alone, even if placed in a nominally 'integrated' school. The primary group encompassed a wide age range (7 to 11 years) so there might have been large differences of view within that group. Seven and 11 year olds are very different from one another in terms of development and school experience so they are likely to differ in their views about school. Seven year olds have been in school a relatively short time. Eleven year olds have around six years' experience of schooling and are, in many school systems, around the age of transfer to secondary schooling and with this, a change in curriculum, classroom organisation and maybe peer and teacher relationships. These potential differences are hidden when results across this broad age range are combined. Further, children who remain in segregated schools might be different (for example, have more behavioural difficulties) from children who are integrated. Barry Wade and Maggie Moore did not follow the same children through primary and secondary school age phases. Instead, different samples of primary and secondary school pupils were used. So, for all these reasons, the authors may not have been comparing like with like when looking at pupils in integrated and segregated settings.

Barry Wade and Maggie Moore used a sentence-completion questionnaire with 160 pupils (this included secondary and primary age groups) to probe attitudes towards schooling. One aspect concerned how the children and young people felt about moving to a different school. In response to the opening statement, 'If I change school I . . .', nearly one-third of the pupils gave what the researchers judged to be positive responses. Just over half the pupils voiced concerns. Changing school does not assume a move between segregated and integrated provision so we cannot interpret these responses as showing support for a particular form of education. However, the level of concerns expressed by pupils does reflect a general conservatism among children in relation to schooling. This type of question, across a range of pupils, has invariably been shown to produce responses supporting the current situation. Children tend to favour the familiar over the unknown.

Some other researchers have interviewed pupils, with emotional or behavioural difficulties, attending special schools or units (Armstrong et al., 1993; Cooper, 1993). One important finding of Derek Armstrong and his co-workers was that adults rarely explained to these pupils (5 to 16 year olds), in terms that the children and young people could understand, what was going on when their special needs were being assessed. The pupils were made to feel powerless because decisions were made about them without the pupils being consulted or informed appropriately.

It is interesting to consider what happens when children move from segregated to integrated schools. Following the same pupils through removes some problems that arise when different groups of children are involved. If we interview children in mainstream schools and a different group in special schools then any differences of view may reflect differences between the children or the schools they happen to attend. Differences may not reflect degree of integration.

Roger Kidd and Garry Hornby (1993) interviewed twenty-nine 8 to 16 year olds who had been transferred from a special (for pupils with moderate learning difficulties (MLD)) school to mainstream schools when the MLD school closed. Over three-quarters (twenty-two) of the pupils were happy with the transfer, four regretted it and three were neutral. However, there was a difference within the sample. There were generally greater levels of satisfaction among the pupils who were transferred to a mainly 'resource-based' school (i.e. in which part of the school day was spent in a specially resourced and staffed classroom, separate from mainstream schoolmates) than where pupils did not have this arrangement. Interestingly, interviews with the parents also showed stronger satisfaction with the resource-based school than with other mainstream school arrangements. Within the latter group, there was more support for a situation in which three ex-MLD school pupils were in the same class than when pupils were placed individually in mainstream school classes.

Things which were liked about mainstream schools included the food, the wider curriculum and the more intensive work. Reservations related to having to wear school uniform and a lack of help with some subjects. Roger Kidd and Garry Hornby do not report any comments (positive, negative or neutral) by the transferred pupils about their teachers, classmates or lives outside school.

The pupils were interviewed just over a year after they had transferred schools and, possibly, would have had different views after a longer time in the mainstream school. It was a small sample and, as in Barry Wade and Maggie Moore's work, combining a wide age range may have hidden systematic differences between older and younger pupils. Nonetheless the work is interesting in following up pupils who had transferred from special schools. It echoes the earlier finding that pupils tend to endorse the current provision, even when change is relatively recent.

VIEWS OF CHILDREN ATTENDING SCHOOLS FOR PUPILS WITH MLD

I talked with fifty-six 9 to 11 year olds, forty-one boys and fifteen girls, attending two schools for pupils with moderate learning difficulties (MLD) to find out what they thought about their mainstream and special schools. (See Lewis, 1995, for further details about samples, methods and coding.) The children also drew pictures of liked and disliked aspects of their schools. Some of these pictures are reproduced later in this chapter alongside the child's commentary. These children made up all the 9 to 11 year olds attending segregated MLD provision in one local education authority (school district). The larger number of boys than girls in this sample is representative of the special school population in

England (DES, 1992). Boys comprised 66 per cent of the full-time special school population in England in 1991 (compared with 73 per cent in the sample interviewed). The bias towards boys in special school populations is also found in other countries (see O'Hanlon, 1993).

Most of the children interviewed had been at their special schools for three to four years. This reflects a tendency for the move to special schools to be at around age 7 when children would otherwise have been moving between infant and junior departments or schools in the mainstream school sector. Two-thirds of the children had attended their current special schools for over one year.

The children had generally good memories for factual information that could be checked. This was the case even though it was as long as seven years since some of these children had attended mainstream schools. Fifty-two of the children named previous (i.e. mainstream) schools. Forty-three of these were named correctly. I cannot tell whether the children genuinely recalled this information from the time of the move or whether they had been told about this subsequently. Most of the children who named the incorrect school gave the name of a mainstream school currently attended by a brother or sister. Another thing about which the children were generally accurate concerned the length of time for which they had attended the MLD school. Forty-three of the fifty children who estimated this were correct (to the nearest three months). Most of the children who gave an incorrect estimate were children who had attended their special schools for just under a year but guessed this to be over a year.

School transfer

Children's recall about the processes of moving schools can tell us something about how involved the children may have been and the kinds of information they were given. Of course it is not possible with retrospective accounts to know how much was gleaned later. Many children (one-third) appeared to have no knowledge of why they had moved schools. This may suggest the children's passivity: that these children accepted, without question, what was being done to them in terms of school placement. Alternatively, the children may have forgotten or denied reasons for school transfer although, as noted earlier, they could generally remember factual details well. This lack of knowledge might also have arisen because adults did not want to be explicit about reasons for moving to special schools in case the information made the children feel that they had failed educationally.

Reasons for transfer

Approximately two-thirds of the children could give one or more reasons why they had left their mainstream schools. It is not possible to know the source of the children's information or misinformation. Inaccurate knowledge about school transfer may have reflected what the child had been told (for example, that the move was due to a medical problem). Unfortunately it was not possible to interview the parents or mainstream school teachers of these children. They may have shed light on why the children gave certain responses.

The children's ideas about why they had been moved from mainstream to special schools can be divided into six broad groups. These are summarised in Figure 1. This shows the percentage of children giving answers in each of the main categories: poor work, age to transfer, an adult's decision, experiencing bullying, misbehaviour or a medical reason. The final bar (the largest single group) represents the children who said that they did not know why they had moved schools. Some children gave several reasons so their responses feature in more than one bar on the graph.

(i) Aspects of themselves   About one-third of the children said that they had moved from mainstream to special schools because of some aspect of their own work, behaviour or health. It is perhaps surprising that only one in five of the children gave 'poor work' as the reason for their move from mainstream to MLD schools as a slower pace of learning and lower level of attainment (compared with peers) is probably the immediate reason for most such transfers. Some children identified particular curricular areas (usually reading) in which they had experienced problems in mainstream schools:

'I had problems with my writing' (Eva, age 11)

'I couldn't write my name . . . but I can now' (Rhys, age 10)

'Poor reading' (Dan, age 10; Ian, age 10; Jo, age 11)

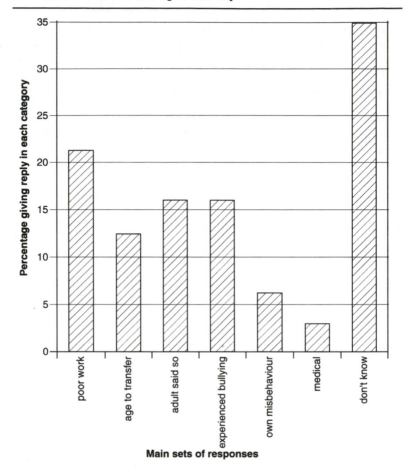

Figure 1 Responses to 'Why did you come to this school?'

'Bad maths' (Alban, age 11)

Other children referred to a general slowness:

'I had to catch up on my work' (Reuben, age 11)

'I was slow' (Del, age 11)

'I was slow at learning' (Briony, age 10)

'Cos I was born backwards . . . only a bit backwards' (Shaun, age 11)

Three children, hinting at the special school as a punishment, said that their misbehaviour in the mainstream school led to transfer:

'I was playing about' (Raoul, age 9)

'I was getting moody' (Viola, age 9)

Implicit in these types of comment is a view that certain aspects of work or behaviour made a child unsuitable for a mainstream school. The comments thus reflect messages, whether justifiable or not, about the children's perceptions of a lack of inclusivity in mainstream schools.

There is evidence that learning and behavioural difficulties overlap, one often leading to the other (Croll and Moses, 1985). Teachers usually cope more readily with children with learning, but not behavioural, difficulties than with children perceived as experiencing both sets of problems. So one might have expected more children to give misbehaviour as the reason for the move out of mainstream schools. However, any experience of disapproval of misbehaviour in schools may have encouraged the children to keep quiet about this subsequently. Thus the children may have chosen to give other reasons even if they suspected misbehaviour to have been an element in their transfer. This may have been why misbehaviour was given as the reason for transfer by only three children, all of whom were in the youngest age group interviewed.

Two children attributed the move to special schools to specific medical factors, for example, epilepsy.

(ii) An adult's wishes or instructions One in six of the children attributed the move from mainstream to special schools to the wishes of an adult. This was usually a parent. Ramon's (age 10) comment was typical of this group: 'My mum said it was best for me'. Comments about a parent suggesting the move to a special school were invariably given in positive terms. Such comments were often backed up with an explanation of why the move would be a good idea. Sometimes the adult suggesting the move was somebody outside the family, such as a psychologist: 'The man [psychologist] said to come' (Melvin, age 10).

(iii) Problems with other children or teachers in mainstream schools A similar proportion (one in six) of the children said that they had moved schools because of difficulties with other children:

'I got called names, "Hob-Nob" and that' (Del, age 11)

'I got picked on' (Nerys, age 10)

'Them other kids kept kicking me so I ran away' (Tessa, age 10)

'I couldn't get on with my work there [mainstream school] cos of the other kids, kept annoying me' (Mervin, age 9)

It is not possible to know whether these reports were accurate. However, the accuracy of these perceptions is not the issue here. If children believe that they were bullied by other children in main-stream schools then this will affect their views of mainstream schools. Bullying and problems with other children are discussed more fully under 'playtimes' later in this chapter.

No child directly attributed the move to a special school to a teacher. However, occasionally there were hints that teachers were to blame for the move, for example through giving the child work that was too difficult.

(iv) Routine transfer   Seven children explained the transfer from mainstream to special schools in terms of a routine move between schools. This move was thought to be due to, for example, the child reaching the last class in one school (e.g. infant–junior transfer at age 7) or a family house move. For example, Roddy (age 9) said, 'I came here cos we moved house'. Similarly, several children said that they had come to the special school because 'I got too old for that [mainstream] school'. For these children, the nature of the school was irrelevant to the reasons for the move. This tied in with age 7 being the most common transfer age for children at the special schools. It is not clear whether the children were rationalising about the move or were genuinely confused and believed that the change of school was compulsory with the exact school being irrelevant or arbitrary.

Most of the reasons for school transfer were positive in the children's eyes. Transfer to the special school was rarely seen explicitly as a punishment or negative in some other way. I also asked the children if they would like to move schools. There was overwhelming support for their current schools with fifty-three out of the fifty-six children interviewed saying that they wished to stay at their special schools.

This support for special schools contrasts with some reports of parents' views. Roger Kidd and Garry Hornby (1993), surveying parents' views after a special school closed and pupils were moved to mainstream schools, found support for the transfer from a majority of the parents. Nineteeen out of twenty-nine parents surveyed were happy with the transfer. A survey of 160 parents of children with special needs in two regions of the UK found that one-third of the parents of children in special schools wanted a change of school (Audit Commission/HMI, 1992). Nearly two-thirds of these parents wanted a change to a mainstream school and a further one-sixth wanted a mix of special and mainstream school placement.

Only three of the fifty-six MLD school children whom I interviewed said that they wanted to move to a mainstream school. These children wanted to go to a mainstream school because their reading had now improved or to be with a particular friend. This endorses the findings of other researchers, reviewed earlier, that children will tend to support their current schools. Possible reasons for children's views are explored next.

Possible reasons for views

The positive evaluations of special schools may be taken at face value. These children had all experienced some degree of academic (usually accompanied by social) difficulties in the mainstream school. This is a common pattern among children with mild or moderate learning difficulties. Consequently, it is perhaps not surprising that the children preferred to be in a school in which those difficulties were less evident, less conspicuous or regarded as less deviant.

The wording of the question may have produced a conservative response. The children were asked if they would like to move schools. Wishing to stay at the current school does not preclude the child from having reservations about that school. Most of the children identified features of special schools that they disliked and these are discussed later in this chapter. Presumably there is likely to be a connection between children's attitude to special school placement and understood reasons for being there. For example, the children who believed that it was a routine organisational move would have been unlikely to expect, or wish, to move at a non-transfer age (for example, between ages 8 and 11). Children who believed that special school placement reflected specific lack of skills may have expected to move back once those skills had been acquired. Many children attributed their move, from mainstream to special school, to the dictate of an adult. Consequently it is possible that only those children who were certain that they wanted to change schools would have said this to an adult interviewer.

SPECIAL AND MAINSTREAM SCHOOLS – LIKED ASPECTS AND RESERVATIONS

Figures 2, 3, 4 and 5 summarise what children from the two MLD schools said in interviews about liked aspects of special and mainstream schools, and, conversely, what was disliked about each setting. The rest of this chapter deals with the main areas by theme. Overall, the curriculum was relatively well liked in both special and mainstream schools. By contrast, the playground was a disliked feature of both settings, particularly mainstream schools.

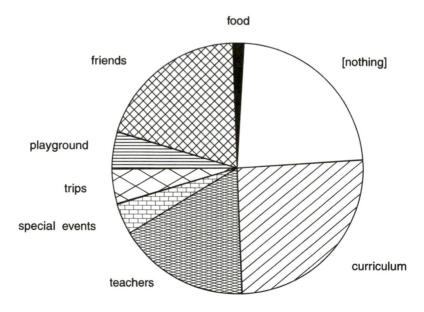

Figure 2 Responses to 'What were the things you liked about x [mainstream school]?'

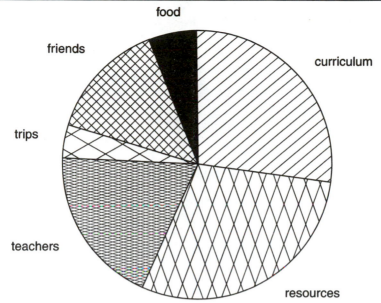

Figure 3 Responses to 'What are the things you like about y [special school]?'

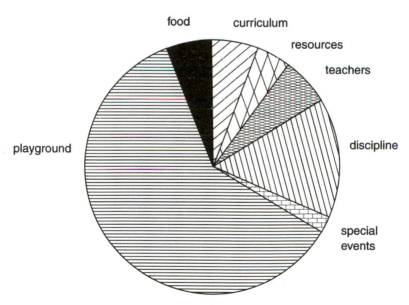

Figure 4 Responses to 'What were the things you didn't like about x [mainstream school]?'

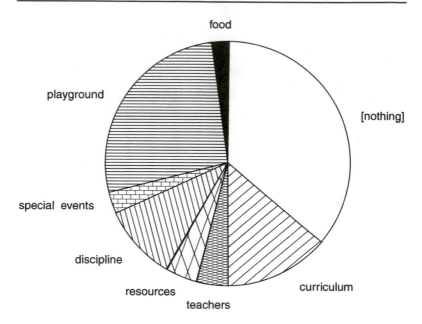

Figure 5 Responses to 'What are the things you don't like about y [special school]?'

Teachers and discipline

Teachers' attitudes are central in determining whether children feel included in, and good about, school. Teachers were mentioned as a positive feature of special and/or mainstream schools by a substantial minority of the children. In general, it was not the same group of children who named teachers as a liked aspect of each setting.

Nearly a quarter (thirteen children) named the teachers as a liked aspect of special schools:

'Mr Quinn [teacher] plays with us and reads us funny stories and he's kind to us and does football' (Melvin, age 10)

'Miss Hart, she's nice she is. My best teacher. She helps me lots' (Becky, age 11)

'Best thing's Mrs Jay cos she's my best friend' (Amy, age 10)

Matthew gave this explanation of the picture in Figure 6:

My mum bring me here [special school] and I saw the teacher. The teacher says I can come to this school if I want but not if I don't want. I don't have to come if I don't want. I can decide for myself. The teacher said she hopes I will come 'cos she thinks I'll have a good time at this school. So I came. The teacher's happy so she's smiling.

Figure 6 Picture by Matthew (age 10) of a teacher at his special school

Ten children named teachers as one of the liked aspects of mainstream schools. Many of these children were recalling incidents with teachers from several years previously, suggesting that these had made a substantial impact on the children. For these children, highlights of mainstream schooling were associated with being made to feel special or successful by a particular teacher or school event and their comments echo those of Donna Williams quoted in Chapter 1:

'Teacher chose me. I was king in the play, not a soldier' (Matt, age 10)

'[Teacher] was nice to me' (Esther, age 10; Coral, age 9)

'I had a [epileptic] fit. The teacher was kind' (Ned, age 10)

'Mrs Fitz [headteacher/principal] like me. She give me stickers' (Jess, age 9)

A sense of humour, kindness and fairness were all mentioned positively as features of 'nice' teachers (from mainstream or special schools). This suggests very similar views to those held by children in mainstream schools (see, for example, Cullingford, 1991).

Just under a quarter of the children gave discipline as a disliked aspect of mainstream and/or special schools.
Ian gave this explanation of his picture in Figure 7:

The teacher [at special school] is shouting at me. Don't like it when she shouts at me.

Ian disliked being shouted at. He depicted this with a disembodied

Figure 7 Picture by Ian (age 10) of his teacher at the special school

teacher's head and emphasis placed on the loud shouting 'sounds' from the mouth.

Some memories of being disciplined in the mainstream school were detailed and vivid even after several years: 'There were these bushes and kids pushed me in the stingers [stinging nettles] and teacher told me off. Had to miss playtimes' (Joe, age 11).

Barry had been at the special school for three years but he still had clear memories of being told off while at his mainstream school. This is illustrated in the picture in Figure 8 in which Barry is on the right and, to the left, the headteacher. Barry has been in trouble and has been sent to stand outside the headteacher's room. He is waiting outside the room for the headteacher to tell him to come in. Barry cannot go in until the green light on the panel next to the door comes on (on the right of the picture). At this point the headteacher has just come out to take Barry into the room. The headteacher's spectacles and beard were remembered very vividly.

Figure 8 Picture of the headteacher at the mainstream school by Barry (age 10) (No commentary)

There is so much detail in this picture that it was possible to verify certain details, such as the lighted panel. There was no such panel in Barry's special school but there had been one in the mainstream school at the time he had attended that school.

Inevitably, discipline was welcomed in some contexts and disliked in others. Some children made comments reflecting a wish for more autonomy and less adult control. For example, several children explicitly preferred special to mainstream schools because they had a choice of dinners at the special school. Opportunities to choose, even if only in the (to many adults) relatively unimportant sphere of dinners, were welcomed. In contrast, the curriculum, particularly in the mainstream school, was not something to be negotiated or chosen.

Playtime

Procedures of school transfer, teachers and discipline relate to the power of adults. Playtimes are the point at which teacher control may be replaced by pupil control. In the playground, the school ethos is tested as the children move out of the immediate range of adults. Many researchers into playground life in primary schools emphasise the importance of the playground as the forum in which children learn the rules of childhood culture. To participate in this world, the child must recognise and work within the particular rules of that world.

Playtime recurs as an issue in many studies of children's views of school. Often it has also been seen as a problem by teachers and strategies for using it productively have been debated. Some countries, for example New Zealand, have issued advice to teachers on using playtimes productively. In the UK, primary school teachers have estimated that just under 10 per cent of children show bullying or spiteful behaviours. In one survey, 8 per cent of 7 to 11 year olds in inner city primary schools admitted to regular bullying (Mortimore et al., 1988). A much wider group may be caught up in playground fights or bullying. Sixty-seven per cent of 6 and 7 year olds reported getting into fights (Tizard et al., 1988). A follow-up study of the same children found little change, with 59 per cent involved in fights at 11 years old (Mooney et al., 1991). How do these findings about mainstream schools in general compare with researchers' conclusions concerning, specifically, children with special educational needs?

Several studies have monitored what happens to children with special needs in mainstream schools at playtimes. These children tend to be isolated in the playground. A recent study found that pupils with marked special needs (i.e. children with a formal statement of their special educational needs) were more likely to be bullied than were other pupils, especially at secondary school level (Nabuzoka *et al.*, 1993). These pupils were also slightly more likely, especially for boys at secondary school, to carry out bullying.

Nearly two-thirds of the MLD school children recalled playtime as a disliked aspect of mainstream schools and associated this with verbal or physical aggression from other children:

> 'Other kids called me names and that in [the] playground ... The children didn't want to be my friend. They called me names like Cherry-Berry, Fatty, Tramp' (Alan, age 9)

> 'In the playground ... the other kids would get on to me all the time ... fighting, kicking' (said individually by Dan, age 10; Benni, age 10; Jo, age 10; Phillip, age 10; Natalie, age 10)

Many children drew pictures of themselves as recipients of fighting and teasing in the playground. Some pictures showed the fighting or name-calling in progress; others depicted the aftermath. When showing the aftermath, children always drew themselves alone.

> 'I got jumped on by loads of kids. Got hurt. Crying'

Clyde drew himself crying. He then wrote 'no' underneath the picture in Figure 9 explaining that this meant 'bad'.

These MLD school children, most of whom were recalling the infant school period, were not unusual in

Figure 9 The aftermath of being bullied in the playground at the mainstream school, by Clyde (age 11)

reporting playground problems. They may have been unusual in being the target of frequent bullying. Alternatively they may not have been bullied more than other children, or even very often. However, they appear to have had difficulties in dealing with aggressive behaviours (verbal or physical) of other children. So it may be the impact, not the frequency, of the bullying that is reflected in these comments. Did these children attract bullying behaviour in some way? Fewer children, but still a substantial minority (a quarter), mentioned playtime at the special school as a source of difficulties. Children who did express anxieties about playtimes there referred to problems from other children, not isolation. Maybe the children had few expectations of cooperation with others and so did not comment on solitary playground play.

'Don't like playtimes [at special school]. Get kicked in playtimes' (said individually by Ivor, age 10; Rupert, age 10; Carmen, age 10)

'Them kids give me battering playtimes' (Bram, age 9)

Autobiographical accounts of adults with learning difficulties also contain many references to problems in school playgrounds. Richard Waller, for example, has described being pushed about by other children until he exploded into a response and defended himself. In retrospect he views this positively and concludes, 'So I learned through my handicaps to take care of myself' (1981: 128).

Children and teachers seem to have different emphases in what they see as constituting worrying playground behaviour among children. Children were concerned about aggression from other children. Teachers were concerned about this but also broader issues such as children's isolation and lack of cooperative games. Teachers at the MLD schools said that they believed the children had difficulties in working with other children. This, they believed, was shown in both the classroom and the playground. This view is supported by research into comparisons of children with learning difficulties in special and mainstream schools (Martlew and Hodson, 1991). How far such difficulties stem from factors within the child and how far they reflect the social context of the behaviour is open to debate. Whatever the cause, it seems that the playground generates negative experiences for many children with learning difficulties. Attempts to develop inclusive schools will need to address what happens in the playground but this needs to be considered as part of the whole school ethos, not just as an isolated matter. This is discussed more fully in Chapter 7.

Friends

If a child feels vulnerable in school, subject to teachers' or other children's power, then friends become an especially important source of defence and support. The view is expressed well by an Australian researcher:

> To be alone in a new place is potentially devastating. To find a friend is partially to alleviate the problem. By building with that friend a system of shared meanings and understandings, such that the world is a predictable place, children take the first step towards being competent people within the social setting of the school.

(Davies, 1982: 63)

Many of the MLD school children, remembering liked aspects of mainstream schools, talked about friends there. One-fifth of these children named friends as a particularly liked aspect of mainstream schools.

> 'This is Karl. He's still my friend even though he knows what school I go to' (Alan, age 11)

Alan drew (see Figure 10) a particular friend, Karl, from his previous school with whom he had remained friends. Alan's comment about Karl implied that Alan had expected his attendance at the MLD school to have ended his friendship with Karl.

None of the children explicitly mentioned lack of friends as a disliked aspect of previous

Figure 10 Karl, Alan's (age 11) friend at the mainstream school

or current schools. However, this was implied in some reactions to, and accounts of, being the subject of playground aggression. This was especially so when in mainstream schools. Only eleven of the children named friends as among liked aspects of the special school. Friends may have tended to be community, rather than school, based. Arguably it was more important to have friends in the mainstream school than in the special school owing to the reported higher frequency of playground aggression in mainstream schools. Several children mentioned the positive and supportive ethos of the special school, in contrast to what they perceived as a harsher environment of mainstream schools:

'Nice children at this school. They share things. Not like in [previous mainstream] school' (Becky, age 11)

'Teachers here are friendly. They stop the naughty children' (Josie, age 10)

It may have been the case that the children's perceptions of a more supportive ethos of the special schools, compared with mainstream schools, made the issue of having friends there less likely to arise. There was a general tendency to view MLD school children as better behaved than children from the mainstream schools, for example not playing up in class so much. This was especially so for children who had moved into the special school relatively recently.

Curriculum

An inclusive school ethos is characterised by curricula that meet the educational needs of the full range of children. A review of published research evidence suggests that liked and disliked aspects of the curriculum tend to be similar for special and mainstream school pupils. Gender and age differences seem to be more significant than are differences based on special/mainstream school. Seven to 11 year olds attending inner city primary schools were reported as liking physical education, painting and reading to themselves. By contrast, story writing and mathematics were comparatively unpopular (Mortimore et al., 1988). Similar rankings were found among 6 and 7 year olds in mainstream schools (Pollard et al., 1994). Julie, a 16 year old with severe learning difficulties, cited friends and work as favoured aspects of school. She communicated, through speech and signing, what she liked to do at school: 'Tasks . . . being with Winston [her friend], cooking, tapes [music]' (Tilstone, 1992b).

One might have anticipated that children in special schools for children with MLD, when asked what they remembered as having disliked about mainstream schooling, would mention the curriculum. However, the MLD school children with whom I talked rarely mentioned work as a disliked aspect of their mainstream schools. Only three children named work as a disliked feature of those schools and, conversely, nearly one child in three gave 'lessons' as something they had positively liked (drawing attention to particular curricular areas, notably swimming and cooking):

'I was good at sounds work' (Rhys, age 10)

'I liked doing numbers' (Ramon, age 10)

'Best thing was swimming' (said individually by Alan, age 9; Eva, age 11; and Lee, age 10)

Pictures of liked aspects of mainstream schools often reflected this enthusiasm for aspects of the curriculum. None of these pictures featured 'core' subjects of reading, writing or mathematics but they did depict swimming, football, art or cookery.

'This is me at my other school. Crayoning and drawing. I liked that' (Joanne, age 10)

Figure 11 shows Joanne with her crayons and completed picture. Like other children's pictures of curricular activities in the mainstream school, it shows the child on her own without other children or the teacher. Looking through these pictures I was reminded of other researchers' conclusions that people with learning difficulties may be rarely alone yet are often lonely (Richardson and Ritchie, 1989).

Perhaps, given its greater immediacy, it was not surprising that the curriculum and associated resources featured strongly in the MLD school children's accounts of both liked and disliked features of their special schools. One child in three named aspects of the curriculum as a liked feature of their special schools. These features encompassed reading, writing, maths, swimming and painting. The single most frequently mentioned aspect was a soft play area (these existed in both special schools). Many children talked in detail about materials and activities in the soft play areas. They were also valued as a source of others' envy. Family, friends and

Figure 11 Enjoying doing work at the mainstream school by Joanne (age 10)

neighbours reportedly wanted 'to have a go' in the soft play or 'ball park' areas. This was illustrated in Nerys's (age 10) remark: 'My friend, Debbie, what goes to [mainstream] school, wants to come to this school and go in our ball park'.

Pride in success at school tasks was illustrated in many children's pictures of a liked aspect of special schools. Debbie's picture of herself alongside a page of 'correct' sums (Figure 12) was typical of the kinds of curriculum-related pictures drawn by the children.

'I do good sums here. Teacher gives me lots of ticks' (Debbie, age 11)

Very few children who depicted aspects of the curriculum placed other children in the picture. Occasionally a teacher was drawn alongside the children themselves. This may reflect the highly individualised nature of work in the special school and the

Figure 12 Debbie (age 11) at her special school with a successful page of sums

children's difficulties (in the teachers' views) in working collaboratively with classmates.

About one in six of the MLD school children said that they disliked the special school curricula:

'Don't like the sums' (Cary, age 11)

'They give you too hard work here' (said individually by Tessa, age 10; Dan, age 10; and Clyde, age 11)

'They make you do writing' (Matthew, age 10)

Fewer children (and not the same individuals) mentioned aspects of the curriculum as a disliked aspect of mainstream schools. This may have reflected the immediacy of curricular difficulties in the special schools, a poor memory for curricular-related features of mainstream schools or perhaps a less strong academic push for these children when in mainstream schools. It may also have reflected the relative insignificance of curricular difficulties compared with other aspects (notably the playground) causing difficulties in mainstream schools.

PERCEIVED SIMILARITIES AND DIFFERENCES BETWEEN SPECIAL AND MAINSTREAM SCHOOL CHILDREN

Nearly two-thirds of the special school children described themselves as different from mainstream school children. The most frequently given basis for this difference was the poorer behaviour of children in mainstream schools (referred to earlier). One child in three gave this explanation. One in six of the MLD school children described themselves as different from children attending mainstream schools because of their own lower attainments. The same proportion gave the source of this difference as something literal – eye or hair colour or clothes worn. The other children interviewed were unable or unwilling to explain why they thought special and mainstream school children were different from one another.

One explanation for this strong sense of difference may have been the rigid boundaries defining special and mainstream school groups. Because the children were in different schools it may have encouraged them to see themselves as very different from one another.

This sense of difference diminished when the children were asked about their predictions for adult lives. Just over half predicted very similar adult lives for special and mainstream school children: to get married, have families, do a variety of jobs ranging from 'cops' (named by all the children), to boxers, bouncers, computer programmers, teachers, bankers and taxi drivers. The bias towards traditionally male jobs probably reflects the larger number of boys than girls interviewed. The other children gave confused answers or said they could not guess what adult lives would be like.

METHODOLOGY

There are inherent difficulties in obtaining fair and accurate responses when interviewing children and these have been well documented. In addition, children with learning difficulties may be unused to being asked for their opinions. (See further reading on interview methodology, with particular reference to interviewing people with learning difficulties.) This was illustrated by a survey of adults with learning difficulties which found that nearly three-quarters of those people had not chosen the colour of their bedroom walls (Williams, 1978). However, 80 per cent of them would have liked to do so. The same survey found that parents and staff considerably underestimated the views of people with learning difficulties. This survey was carried out some time ago and perhaps these findings would not apply today.

When I talked with the children from MLD schools I did not go back and ask them the same questions again. So I did not discover whether they would have given the same answers on different occasions. I also did not try to trick them by asking the same question more than once. The children may have been saying what they thought I, as the interviewer, wanted to hear. Also, they may have been giving replies to questions, even if they had little understanding of the question, because they thought that giving any answer would be better than saying nothing. What they said may also have been influenced by recent events, such as a telling off in the playground or praise for particular work. Children may also have been influenced by other children's reports of their discussions. All these reservations need to be borne in mind when interpreting the children's responses.

Despite these cautions there are similarities with the findings of other researchers who have investigated mainstream school children's views. There are also consistencies with the small amount of published work relating to the views of children with special educational needs. Interviews with the children's friends, brothers, sisters and neighbourhood playmates would have been interesting and may have provided insights into why the MLD school children held particular views.

Several researchers have drawn up guidelines for interviewing people with learning difficulties (see further reading). They are also relevant, more widely, to any conversation in which the views of people with learning difficulties are being sought. Points made include:

- use open questions that give the person being interviewed scope to develop the answer in their own way;
- avoid questions that require yes or no answers only;
- avoid questions that require very precise answers;
- be flexible about how questions are asked, for example changing the order of questions for different interviewees but check that this will not bias answers;
- ask questions in several ways; check that this does not change the meaning of the question (for example, changing 'What did

you like about your other school?' to 'What was the best thing about your other school?');

- involve a range of different ways of responding, for example including some ways of physically manipulating a scale (such as moving a pointer along a board); then compare answers given when questions have required different ways of responding.

CONCLUSION

The views of schooling held by young MLD school children are broadly similar to those found by other researchers to be held by children in mainstream primary schools. A significant difference between special and mainstream school pupils' views may lie in the children's knowledge about, and ability to respond to, the complex web of power structures among children in the classroom and playground. Being unable to cope well with children in the mainstream school playground may have led the special school children into an over-reliance on teachers. Perhaps the special school teachers' vigilance made special school playgrounds a happier place for most of these children than, at least in their recollections, had been the mainstream school playgrounds. Positive experiences with teachers, in mainstream or special schools, were very salient and often recounted in detail.

There can be little doubt about the very positive feelings that most of these children expressed about their special schools. However, these children's worlds did not begin and end at the school gates. Beyond those, the children needed not just specific friends but also the skills of making and keeping friendships. One group of researchers (Jahoda et al., 1988) found that two-thirds of the mentally retarded adults interviewed reported childhood teasing by non-disabled children; all interviewees said that they still experienced teasing or feelings of rejection by the non-disabled. So bullying and teasing are not issues only for schools but extend into the whole community. Arguably the best way to deal with these is not in a contrived way through, for example, specific curricular packages, but by creating natural opportunities for interaction. This was central to the rationale behind the link projects that are discussed in the following chapters.

Chapter 3

Moving towards an inclusive ethos

The link schemes stemmed from the shared convictions of the adults involved. These convictions rested on the view that education should be concerned with more than the acquisition of subject knowledge. The staff believed that education should equip children, socially and emotionally, for living harmoniously with people different from themselves. One mechanism to foster this was to arrange for pupils to work with a more diverse group of children and young people than those found within each school. This chapter looks at preparatory work for the link schemes, how sessions were planned, adults' roles and resource issues. More generally, the chapter examines research evidence about, and associated strategies for, fostering positive attitudes towards disabled people, developing children's understanding of disability. Some strategies for building up communication skills likely to be important in integrated classrooms are also reviewed.

Each link scheme encompassed overlapping goals for the special and mainstream schools. For staff from the special schools, specific aims included aiding children and young people with severe learning difficulties to develop a range of strategies that would help them to build relationships. These staff also wanted to develop their pupils' awareness of the needs of others. For staff from mainstream schools, specific aims included giving their pupils an insight into the lives of disabled children and young people. These insights were to come through working with children and young people from special schools.

Similar goals have been put forward in a variety of link schemes and also in handicap awareness programmes in which pupils from mainstream schools are taught about disability. The Mental Handicap Awareness' project reported by John Quicke and his co-workers (Quicke *et al.*, 1990) includes a review of that project's underlying principles. The principles, which have implications for special and mainstream school pupils, were:

- children and adults with a mental handicap are individuals;
- children and adults with a mental handicap are not passive objects of charity;
- the families of a child with a mental handicap are 'normal';
- the 'natural' location of all people with a mental handicap is not an institution;
- people with a mental handicap are not a clearly identifiable group;
- no one professional group has a monopoly of knowledge in this area.

WORKING WITH PARENTS

Judith Snow, a disabled person who has worked extensively in developing inclusive schools, has drawn attention to parents' needs:

> The school must become a place of welcome for parents as well as children, assisting them in strengthening their abilities to dream, to work for inclusion despite many barriers, and to contribute to the making of an inclusive school.
>
> (quoted in O'Brien *et al.*, 1989: 12)

This emphasises the impact of an inclusive ethos on the school community as a whole. When developing an inclusive ethos in mainstream schools the impact on parents of both special and mainstream school pupils needs to be considered.

The Link 7 and Link 11 projects were discussed in workshops, both before and during the work, with parents of the special school pupils involved. Several of these parents made the point that through the link projects they had come to recognise what children, of their son's or daughter's age, who were attending mainstream schools could do in school. Parents reacted in contrasting ways to this knowledge. For some, it was the spur to press for increased time in mainstream schools for their children. For other parents, it represented another phase in recognising their child's strengths and limitations compared with other children. Fathers, in particular, had often had little contact with children outside the immediate family and did not know how their children compared with others. Without this knowledge they found it difficult to make decisions about their child's education or to be clear about their role in this. Several commentators have reported the isolation of fathers of children with special needs (Yura, 1987; Herbert and Carpenter, 1994). The traditional caring roles and links with various professionals concerned with children with special needs have tended to be taken by mothers. The type of parent support group attached to link and other integration schemes may therefore be particularly valuable as a strategy for reaching fathers of children with special needs.

More broadly, Sue Wood (1988) has provided an interesting critique of partnership between parents and professionals in the special needs context. It is thought provoking to read this alongside others' suggestions for practice as she prompts questions about the roles and value positions in such partnerships. John O'Brien and his co-workers (1989), Garry Hornby (1991), Phillipa Russell (1991) and Sheila Wolfendale (1992) are among those who have made suggestions about working with families of disabled children, particularly in relation to integration. Advice includes talking with parents about:

- the family's history, interests, needs and likes;
- the gifts of their child with special needs;
- what hopes and dreams they hold for the child;
- their fears or nightmares for the child;
- the risks, costs and benefits of inclusion.

John O'Brien and his co-workers urge that the child's views are included in family discussions as much as possible. Similarly, brothers and sisters should be involved, either as part of these discussions or subsequently.

Parents of children attending mainstream schools were, like parents of pupils at the special schools, very positive about the link schemes. The only complaint was from a parent who objected because her daughter, attending the mainstream school, was not involved.

How schools introduce parents to special–mainstream school links is complex and a matter for individual schools to decide. These links are more likely to be welcomed if that, or a previous, school has already developed an explicitly inclusive ethos. Specific strategies will reflect local and family circumstances.

PREPARING STAFF – WHOLE SCHOOL POLICY

Children may be taken through preparatory programmes concerning integration and observed carefully to try to ensure that they respond positively to the experiences. However, groundwork with adults may take place incidentally, if at all. Adults may not have the chance to explore their attitudes and understanding. Some of the repercussions of misguided teacher attitudes is illustrated in the comments, reported by Mary McCormack (1992), of a headteacher (principal) of a special school. Pupils from this school spent part of the week in mainstream schools. The special school headteacher recounted how a teacher from the mainstream school picked up a child with Down's syndrome 'because he's so affectionate' and let this child have a short sleep in the middle of the afternoon. This angered the special school headteacher because it contrasted with the approach taken by the child's special school teachers. They were struggling to teach the child to be as 'normal' as possible. If staff in special and mainstream schools can share in discussion about such assumptions it should help to acknowledge and so prevent these kinds of double standards, which may be inappropriate, from developing.

Preparation of staff for creating or developing an inclusive ethos needs to include all members of the school community. A classroom ancillary from a mainstream school involved in a link project told me of her sleepless nights before the first session. She had anticipated that all children from the special school would be incontinent. She had not spoken of this fear to anyone for several months as she had felt embarrassed by her ignorance. This shows the importance of establishing a continuing education programme on handicap awareness for adults alongside developments within the school.

The role and views of parents working as informal helpers in the classroom may be overlooked. In one of the mainstream schools involved here parent helpers, who had routinely worked with the class prior to the link project, declined to work in that class during link sessions. This problem could have been tackled through induction programmes involving everyone directly involved or, if possible, the whole school. It would have been useful if these programmes had incorporated, for everyone, visits to the special school.

School governing bodies (similar to governing boards/school boards) will also need to be involved in fostering an inclusive ethos. A range of specific issues arises such as, at what point mainstream and special school managing bodies merge; and budgetary decisions about how, and where, monies are allocated.

In mainstream schools staff and governors may need to consider strategies for preparing children for the death of a child they have known from the special (SLD) school. The death of a pupil occurs more often in special than in mainstream schools. Early deaths of these pupils may be due to a terminal illness or to limited life expectancies of children with certain types of disability. (In 1989 in the UK the main causes of deaths of 5 to 14 year olds were: congenital abnormalities (11 per cent), diseases of nervous and sense organs (10 per cent), neoplasms (18 per cent) and accidents (38 per cent) (addendum to Glassock and Rowling, 1992).) In some areas medical support staff provide advice to teachers about helping other children come to terms with the death of a child. A number of books and other resource materials are available to help children and teachers deal with related issues (see further reading on bereavement and children). Some recommendations, by workers in bereavement counselling, for teachers helping children to deal with the death of a classmate are:

- watch for changes in children's behaviour such as withdrawal, anger or sullenness; handle these with patience and do not be cross with the child;
- find time to listen when children want to talk about bereavement;
- do not discourage children from talking about a child who has died;
- be ready for questions and always be honest; a teacher must be prepared to say 'I don't know';
- with brothers or sisters of a child who has died, it is important to know about the family's cultural background; do not say anything to children which would confuse them or conflict with messages given by the family;
- show children that it is not shameful to cry;
- be sensitive to what may be special days, such as the birth date of a child who has died;
- keep up routines.

The mainstream school environment

Many writers (including Ashman and Conway, 1989; Stainback and Stainback, 1990, 1992; Lewis, 1991; Beveridge, 1993; Gross, 1993) have identified important features in positive learning environments for pupils with learning difficulties. These characteristics include:

- a differentiated curriculum which makes it possible for pupils with special needs to participate (for example, planning parallel activities at varying levels of difficulty);
- variation of teaching methods so that all pupils with special needs can access, or respond to, activities (for example, listening to taped instructions or recording answers on audio tape instead of writing responses);
- appropriate recognition of, and praise for, success;
- encouragement of cooperation between pupils;
- the development of children's self-monitoring and self-evaluation;
- fostering of children's independence and autonomy in learning;
- effective collaboration between adults;
- effective use of resources;
- a problem solving approach to teaching so that children with special needs are seen as a stimulus, not an impediment, to teacher development.

However, whole school policies and attention to the above aspects are not in themselves sufficient to ensure a school climate that welcomes and responds to pupil diversity. John O'Brien and his co-workers (1989) identified nine common misconceptions that teachers held about pupils with special needs. These included beliefs that pupils with special needs:

- fall well outside the range of differences the teacher in a mainstream school can accommodate;
- learn very little, even with special help;
- require constant adult attention, so need small classes;
- drain the teacher's energy;
- demand so much attention that other children 'lose out';
- need highly specialised approaches;
- will be rejected by non-disabled pupils;
- are better off with 'their own kind';

- already receive a disproportionate amount of educational resources.

In addition, staff in special schools may hold beliefs which curtail
the development of involvement in mainstream schools (Fathers,
1994). These views include beliefs that integration will be associated with:

- the dispersal, and hence diminution, of expertise, funding and
  staff cohesion;
- the reduction in specialist in-service provision related to pupils
  with special needs;
- demands for a minority of staff to be involved in continuous
  supervision of some pupils with special needs during breaks
  and dinner times;
- inadequate curricular differentiation in mainstream schools;
- notional 'integration' based on placing pupils in unresponsive
  mainstream schools and so ultimately being more detrimental
  than segregation.

Preparation for developing an inclusive ethos will need to explore
whether such views are held, whether they are justifiable and, if so,
address the concerns.

An interesting feature of the Link 7 and Link 11 projects was the
way in which they became a source of discussion for all staff in the
schools. This happened formally through in-service sessions
(usually open to all staff including nursery nurses and classroom
ancillaries) and informally through staffroom discussion. For
example, on one occasion a teacher (from the mainstream school),
who was not directly involved in the project, was taking a PE lesson
in the school hall when the children from the special school arrived.
These children walked through the hall on their way to the link
project classroom. After the children from the special school had
walked through the hall, this teacher asked the class she was
teaching what they had noticed about the visiting children. After a
long pause, one child answered, 'One boy was wearing glasses'.
The teacher appeared to expect the children to comment on something 'different' about the special school children; otherwise, why
ask the question? Her class seem to have noticed nothing unusual
and appear to have been puzzled by the question. Eventually the
only exceptional feature was deemed to be an immediately observ-
able difference, that one child wore glasses.

This incident generated much discussion among both mainstream and special school staff about why the teacher had asked the question, what she and other teachers would have expected children to reply, and what the child's response said about his or her perceptions. This discussion was valuable in highlighting the teacher's assumptions and ways in which teachers may inadvertently pass on inappropriate expectations to children.

One result of such indirect whole school involvement was that children from the special schools were subsequently integrated full time into the mainstream schools in which they had worked. Some went into mainstream school classes of teachers who, prior to the link projects, had voiced profound reservations about working with SLD school pupils. The link schemes also enabled teachers to experience integrated classes in a supportive context and then to develop integration independently. The large number of mainstream and special school pupils working together in these projects was atypical. The later integration was more natural in that it involved individuals or very small groups of children being integrated but this would not have happened without the link schemes.

PREPARING PUPILS

Preparing pupils (from special and mainstream schools) for integration can be considered from the point of view of attitudes (what feelings do we want to promote?), knowledge (what information is needed to foster understanding and acceptance?) and communication skills (what do children need in order to be able to communicate with one another?). In practice, preparatory activities will be likely to affect more than one of these elements. For example, a non-disabled child role-playing a disabled person may gain both knowledge (for example, where the normal field of vision falls for a person in a wheelchair) and understanding of feelings (such as irritation at being addressed through another person 'Does she. . .', 'Can he. . .'). Attitudes and knowledge will be considered separately in order to draw out, first, what is known from relevant theoretical work, and second, associated strategies for practice. The theoretical work predominantly concerns non-disabled children as there has been relatively little research exploring either the attitude development of children with severe learning difficulties or their concepts of ability and disability.

Fostering positive attitudes to disabled people – findings from research evidence

One of the aims of the link projects (for special and mainstream schools) was to foster understanding and acceptance of others. Various research has pointed to some common findings in developing children's understanding of, and positive attitudes towards, other people (see further reading on children's attitudes towards, and understanding of, disability). Nine findings and their implications are summarised below.

(i) The familiar is preferred over the unfamiliar Visibility of disabled people is important if positive attitudes are to be fostered. This makes it vital to include people with disabilities in a wide range of routine contacts, such as working in shops and appearing in the media. Interestingly, although mail order catalogues in the USA often include pictures of people with disabilities, this is very rare in UK catalogues. This change in UK catalogues would be a small contribution to making people with various disabilities more familiar to the non-disabled.

(ii) The more functionally disabling a disability, the stronger the negative attitudes towards people with that disability In general, the more limiting a disability is seen to be, the more negatively the disabled individual is viewed. Consequently it is important to highlight individuals' abilities, not their disabilities. Autobiographical accounts by people with disabilities are one way of drawing attention to strengths and the whole person. These de-emphasise both disability as a deviation from the norm and disability as the defining characteristic of a disabled person.

(iii) Visibility of disability seems to be a factor in acceptance In general, more visible disabilities are seen more negatively than are the less visible. This association is stronger for attitudes held by younger (i.e. nursery/infant school age) than for upper primary/secondary age children. The association between visibility of the disability and negative attitudes is likely to decrease in significance as children have more contact with the disabled person(s).

(iv) Children who have had little contact with disabled people are more accepting of people with disabilities in school, than in home or community, situations This finding may be a reflection of broader social unease in the community. It suggests that contact with disabled people in school will provide a good starting point for developing positive attitudes towards the disabled.

(v) In general, structured contact with disabled people has led children to have more positive attitudes towards those people than occurs with unstructured contact If children are left to mix in an unstructured way (for example, at playtime (recess/break) only) then the benefits, in terms of increased acceptance, tend not to occur as widely as they do through structured contact. A review of research concluded that,

> The small amount of published research indicates that integration between students with severe and multiple learning difficulties and their peers will not take place of its own accord, but will only be achieved through the continued provision of structured opportunities.
>
> (Jenkinson, 1993)

A range of work has suggested that the form of structure which is most productive is collaborative working, as contrasted with individualistic (each doing his or her own thing) or competitive contexts.

(vi) Other factors likely to affect non-disabled children's acceptance of disabled people include those people's communication difficulties, unusual behaviours and interpersonal skills (particularly impression management) This indicates that both disabled people and the non-disabled need to be taught how to make the most of attempts to communicate with one another.

(vii) Attitudes towards known disabled groups are generalised to less well-known groups This suggests that adults need to beware of inadvertently reinforcing stereotypes and over-generalisations about disability. An antidote is for children to know and work with people with a variety of disabilities.

(viii) Competent children tend to be seen more positively than are less competent children This may be one reason behind the disproportionate percentage of children with special educational needs, found to be among the recipients of bullying in a recent UK study (Nabuzoka *et al.*, 1993). However, various researchers have found that mainstream school children are more tolerant of a child who is not expected to perform well than they are of a child for whom there is no obvious explanation for relative lack of attainment (Budoff and Siperstein, 1978; Maras, 1993). This may explain the attitudes of Link 7 mainstream school children. They were much more sympathetic to special school children than they were towards full-time classmates with mild learning difficulties.

(ix) Categorised contact (i.e. when the disabled group is clearly labelled as such, as in link projects) is more effective than decategorised contact (i.e. when differences between the disabled and the non-disabled are less obvious) in developing and generalising positive attitudes This is a fascinating finding and one which, at first, seems to run counter to intuition. It has been explored by Pamela Maras and Rupert Brown (1992) who have placed changes in non-disabled children's attitudes towards disabled people in the theoretical context of group processes (see Hewstone and Brown, 1986). Pamela Maras (1993) has discussed the limitations of the 'contact hypothesis' which (crudely) suggested that contact with a minority group will be associated with more positive attitudes towards that group. Clearly contact alone is not enough, so sorting out what it is about the social contact which promotes positive attitudes is important both theoretically and in relation to the implications for practice. It seems that labelling someone as a member of a group, and being very clear about that, will lead to the generalisation of attitudes towards that person. If they are not seen as a member of a group, then the attitudes held are specifically about that person, not the group they represent. For example, having a friend who is in the police will not change negative attitudes towards the police in general, only to that individual. However, if that friend is seen strongly as a member of the police (for example, playing in a police sports team) then it is much more likely that positive views will be held about the police in general, not just that one individual. However, a negative spin-off from this position is that contact between clearly identifiably separate and different groups may increase anxieties of one group about the other. This suggests that the context in which the groups meet is crucial. Taking this back to the link project situation – the school ethos will be critical.

Fostering positive attitudes to disabled people – materials and strategies

If all children are welcomed in the school and pupil differences are recognised and valued then specific programmes to encourage tolerance without patronising disabled people will probably be minimal or unnecessary. This applies to both special and mainstream schools. An unusual account shows how children in a special school responded to the arrival of Ann, a girl with autism. When Ann started at the school, the headteacher asked the other children to be kind and helpful towards Ann. After about six weeks the children had become so enthusiastic about helping Ann that they gave her too much help. The headteacher then had to emphasise to the other children that Ann could do more than they were allowing her to do. They were told that they must fuss less, just let her know that she was one of them and that 'she belonged' (Copeland and Hodges, 1976: 86). This advice was reportedly sufficient to readjust the balance between helpfulness and overprotection.

The following strategies have been used by mainstream schools wishing to foster a more inclusive ethos. This has often included working with pupils from special schools. The ideas overlap with a range of work in the field of personal and social education and are applicable to all pupils, whatever their educational setting. The strategies move from the general to the more specific. The common threads in the materials and approaches can be summarised as aiming to develop:

- respect for individuals
- recognition of similarities
- recognition of differences
- celebration of differences
- celebration of similarities

Personal and social development programmes

Much work in the field of personal and social education is oriented to fostering self-esteem and respect for individuals. It is too extensive to be reviewed adequately here (see, Lang, 1988; Galloway,

1989; Tattum and Tattum, 1992). Examples of approaches include group discussions using specific starter questions to prompt an understanding of others' needs. Such questions include:

What does a friend do?
What makes a good friend?
Who needs/does not need help and why?
What is special about a best friend?

When do you need help, and why?
What do you like to do on your own, and why?
What makes you feel brave?
What makes you feel scared?

What makes you feel fed up?
What makes you feel good?

These ideas overlap with suggestions under the umbrella term of 'circle time'.

Circle time and related approaches

Jenny Mosley (1991, 1993, 1994), who uses the term 'circle time' to describe a range of supportive discussion techniques, has made similar recommendations. These include the following:

- whenever a problem arises in the classroom the children sit in a circle. Once the circle has formed, the whole group discusses ways to solve the problem.
- children sit in a circle at the end of the day, each child says 'I enjoyed ..', 'I did not like ..', 'It was nice when ..', etc., and completes the sentence about their day in school. The authors note that the sessions should try to end with positive statements.
- children sit in a circle not touching one another and with eyes closed. A chosen child touches another who then leaves the group. The other children, keeping their eyes shut, ask the first child questions about the child who has left, such as 'Does he/she have blue eyes?' After, say, three questions the children guess the identity of the child who left the group. If the correct child is not named then questions and guesses continue.

There are various techniques for involving every child in these types of activity in ways that are more interesting than just asking children to speak in turn. For example, a ball of wool could be rolled across the circle, the receiving child makes a statement and rolls the ball of wool on to a child who has not spoken. Children who do not wish to speak can 'pass'. Eventually a complex criss-cross pattern of wool is created linking all the children.

The following ideas are more specifically related to developing understanding of the feelings and needs of disabled people.

Map exercise

A well-used approach, stimulated by Canadian work (see Pearpoint *et al.*, 1992), is based on the idea of drawing a map about a specific individual. The map is described using a metaphor of a kaleidoscope – a mysterious and beautiful tool that changes constantly. The picture is unique and formed by individuals coming together; it is more than each can do alone. In making the map, a disabled person or people who know him or her well answer some key questions about the individual. A facilitator asks the questions and a recorder writes the responses on a large sheet of paper. The following example concerns Katie. Key questions include:

- What is Katie's story? That is, what are the key events in her life?
- What is Katie's dream?
- What is Katie's nightmare?

The originators of this idea suggest that a large outline sketch of a person (Katie in this example) be drawn to help collate responses to the next series of questions which are answered by a number of people who know the person well:

- Who is Katie?
- What are Katie's gifts, strengths and talents?
- What are Katie's needs?

As ideas are offered from individuals they can be written on pieces of paper and glued to the outline shape. Later the ideas can be re-grouped to draw out common themes.

The same approach can be used with special school pupils who collect information about mainstream school pupils. They may do this from video tapes, audio tapes, letters and pictures exchanged between pupils at mainstream and special schools, perhaps before any visits are made.

Circle of friends

Another idea stemming from Canadian work (Pearpoint *et al.*, 1992) is based on empathy. It begins with the question to a group of people who know the target person, 'How would you feel if you were that person?' The group then pools ideas about what that individual may need in terms of social contacts and acts as a support group to the individual. Through discussion a series of tasks for individuals in the support group is identified. For example, in the school context some children might volunteer that if they were Katie they would feel:

> lonely at playtime
> puzzled in maths lessons
> sad at weekends with no one from school to play with

These might in turn lead specific children to volunteer to:

> play with Katie at playtime
> check that she understands her maths tasks
> go to her home at weekends to take her to Brownies

Games

Some teachers have devised board games in which the life events of an individual, depicted through picking up a 'chance card', cause the player to suffer penalties or receive bonuses. Examples of 'chance cards' include:

> learn to drive – move forward three squares
> a friendly neighbour moves next door – move forward six squares
> eyesight begins to fail – move back four squares
> fall down stairs – move back one square

A different type of game overlaps with role play. John Quicke and his co-researchers (1990) give an example used in their work with pupils of secondary school age. The aim of this game was to put a non-disabled child into the position of someone receiving incomprehensible messages and so to understand the senses of confusion and frustration that may be felt by a person with learning difficulties. Two children went outside the room while the remaining group renamed various objects (e.g. bag, ball, table, blackboard, chalk, pen, book) in the room. When the new names had been agreed the two excluded children were brought back in and given instructions like 'Put the ball on the bag'. These two children inevitably made many errors because what they thought of as, for example, a ball had been renamed 'chalk', while the 'bag' was what they thought of as a 'table'. The originators of this idea suggest that subsequent discussion might include how it feels to be handicapped, how others respond to a handicapped person, how others might help and what strategies should be avoided.

Role play and simulation

Teachers have devised simulations in which children play the roles of, for example, a person in a wheelchair who wishes to visit a relative, go to the dentist or watch a football match. Similarly, children may role-play someone who is forgetful or anxious when carrying out routine tasks such as shopping or cooking. Discussion after the role play draws out children's expectations and feelings about disability. More unusual ideas include wearing goggles to simulate visual impairment, wearing industrial gloves to simulate motor impairment and focusing on mirror images when writing to simulate visual impairment or learning difficulties.

More broadly, John Quicke and his co-workers have described the use of theatre groups in a mental handicap awareness project with pupils at mainstream secondary schools.

Film/video

In the link schemes described here the mainstream school and special school children watched videos of other children involved in similar link schemes. For the special school pupils these videos included pupils from their own schools, so after seeing the video material the pupils could ask the children viewed about their experiences. It is a good idea to make videos of link or integration work as the material may be appropriate for use with a range of groups including children from segregated schools, parents and school governors.

A particular value of video material is that it permits non-disabled children to stare at disabled people in a socially acceptable context. To do this in real life is obviously, and as reported in many autobiographical accounts by disabled people, a source of embarrassment to those being watched. Sheenagh Hardie has described how it felt to be on the receiving end of so much staring:

> People stare and stare at us [people with Down's syndrome] – I don't know what they expect to see. I think *they* are odd . . . I don't like people who stare. They are ignorant and make me feel like a freak, something to be ridiculed or laughed at. They don't realise that I am sensitive and have feelings . . . Lots of children stare but they are mostly curious . . . Some people don't know how to speak to me and tend to direct questions to mum or dad instead of me.
>
> (1991: 15, 63)

Jenny Corbett, Elaine Jones and Sue Ralph (1993) have described their collaborative experiences in making a video. The video showed disabled women who, because of their involvement from the start, were presented in ways in which they wished to be portrayed. Their account contains many valuable points for schools wishing to make similar videos.

There are many commercially available videos concerning disabled people (see list of resources concerned with the promotion of positive attitudes towards disabled people). However, these will probably not feature the immediate locality of the children's community as happens with the type of home-made videos used in the link projects.

First-hand accounts

Known children with disabilities may be invited to talk to other children about their experiences. This could be introduced through children in special and mainstream schools writing to one another. Subsequent discussion can draw out the kinds of areas summarised earlier in relation to the map, circle of friends and role play / simulation activities.

There have been some interesting reviews of research into the best way of fostering positive attitudes (see further reading on children's attitudes towards, and understanding of, disability). On balance, direct involvement with disabled people seems to be more effective than indirect methods (reading about them, role-playing) in fostering both empathy and understanding. However, there is a place for indirect methods as a preliminary to contact. The workers in the mental handicap awareness project, referred to earlier, concluded that a lengthy preparatory phase of non-contact between mainstream school pupils and people with mental handicap was essential to successful direct contact. These researchers found that contact without sufficient preparation led to inappropriate behaviour from mainstream school pupils.

Schools could build up scrapbooks on children who will be joining the class. The scrapbooks could contain letters, photographs, favourite pictures, etc., sent from one school to the other before the children meet. Similarly, these types of material could be pasted into a large 'floor book' to be shared by all the children.

Packs

There are packs of materials (see list of resources concerned with the promotion of positive attitudes towards disabled people) which are useful in the early stages of developing an inclusive ethos. They emphasise the individuality of people with disabilities and, often using photographs or autobiographical accounts, prompt children to explore their feelings about disabled people. They contain compilations of ideas and materials drawing on a range of those broad areas given above.

Books

Packs may contain or be supplemented by books about people with disabilities. The appropriate material will clearly vary by age group. Younger children may enjoy stories such as *Don't Forget Tom* (Larsen, 1974) (used in the Link 7 project) to stimulate discussion and questions about learning difficulties. Older children may enjoy *Welcome Home, Jellybean* (Shyer, 1980) also focusing on learning difficulties (used in the Link 11 project). Similar materials are *My Brother Barry* (Gillham, 1981), *The Bus People* (Anderson, 1989), *The Four of Us* (Beresford, 1981) and *Ben* (Shennan, 1980).

These packs and books overlap with approaches in the following section which focus on conveying knowledge about disability. Mal Leicester has provided a useful checklist of twelve points concerning possible bias about disability in books and other learning resources. She asks:

– do the materials show a variety of life styles?

- do they show regard for, and acceptance of, people with disabilities?
- are people with disabilities featured as part of everyday life?
- are there characters with whom special children could identify?
- are such characters portrayed in a positive manner?
- do they show evidence of the ability to make decisions about their own lives?
- is there evidence of stereotyping concerning people with disabilities?
- does the language convey prejudice ('four eyes' 'dumbo' etc.)?
- are events seen only from the able-bodied viewpoint?
- are people with disabilities blamed for their conditions?
- are people with disabilities patronised?
- is the image of the able or able-bodied as having all the power reinforced (through text or illustrations)?

(Leicester, 1992: 86–7)

Children's knowledge of disability – findings from research evidence

Many autobiographical accounts by disabled people contain anecdotes that illustrate the misunderstandings about disability held by the non-disabled. There was a recent radio report, probably untrue, about a visually impaired woman who, accompanied by her guide dog, visited an unfamiliar town. When the woman asked a passer-by for directions, she heard the passer-by walking away. The woman was about to ask somebody else when the passer-by returned and said, 'It's all right, I've told your dog where to go.'

Comparable misunderstandings experienced by people who have difficulty communicating are, by definition, less likely to be recounted. For that reason the autobiographical accounts of Donna Williams (who has autism) (1992), Sheenagh Hardie (who has Down's syndrome) (1991) and contributors to collections of autobiographical writing by people with learning difficulties (included in Orlansky and Heward, 1981; Rieser and Mason, 1990; Atkinson and Williams, 1990) are particularly valuable.

Children's understanding of disability must come at least in part from the adults (in the family, community and school) around them. So it is worrying that various studies have revealed that many adults have a poor understanding of the nature of learning difficulties. One study (Weir, 1981) found that 'most adults' confused physical disability and mental handicap. There is also evidence that adults often confuse mental disability with mental illness (MORI, 1982). Interestingly, a 1993 UK survey of attitudes to mental illness found widespread tolerance alongside misunderstanding (Cole, 1993). Ninety-two per cent of the 2000 people surveyed said that society needed to adopt a more tolerant attitude towards the mentally ill. Mental illness was not well understood. One-third of the adults surveyed believed that mental illness was transparent. These respondents were equating all mental illness with certain sub-types, such as extreme paranoia. These types of misunderstanding prompted the Department of Health to issue an explanatory booklet for the general public (Department of Health, 1993) which outlined different types and degrees of mental illness.

Children of secondary school age have also been found to confuse mental disability, mental handicap and physical disability (Kyle and Davies, 1991). Their misunderstandings mirror those reportedly held by adults. Non-disabled teenagers described someone with a mental handicap as 'a person who is not normal', and 'mad, not all there'. By comparison someone who was mentally ill was described as 'a person who would want to kill someone and can't stop themselves', and 'someone who has a brain trouble so they have a deformed face' (1991: 103). One-third of the fifty-three 13 to 15 year olds interviewed thought that mental handicap and mental illness were the same thing. The prevalence of adults' and young adults' misunderstandings about disability makes it imperative that such views are not passed on to younger children.

Children may hold misunderstandings about disability because they have been explicitly misinformed by adults or have picked up incorrect information. However, misunderstandings may also arise just because the children are too immature, cognitively, to understand some aspects of disability. It is easier to understand what can be seen than what is not seen and, as noted earlier, some types of 'invisible' disability are still misunderstood by some adults.

Children who live with a disabled person may be thought to be unlikely to misunderstand central aspects of that disability. However, John Hull's (1990) account of his experiences of blindness illustrates some of his children's misunderstandings. Thomas, at 3 years old, had an imperfect understanding of what it meant to be without sight. For example, when Thomas and his father read/listened to a story together using a book and accompanying audio cassette, Thomas said, 'Thomas wants the light, Thomas can't see without the light' (1990: 32). John Hull inferred from this that Thomas believed that his father did not need a light because he could see the book in the dark. Imogen, age 10½, had a more accurate understanding of blindness but still had some misconceptions. She was confused about the onset of John's blindness believing, correctly, that he could see when he was a child. However, Imogen apparently forgot, despite recent conversations about previous joint activities requiring John to see, that he had also had some vision for much of her early childhood.

The primary or elementary school spans a period when most children's knowledge about others develops rapidly. Five, 7 and 11 year olds differ in terms of what they say is important in others' behaviours and how these features are interpreted. A 5 year old will tend to describe a friend as fair haired and wearing a red dress. However, a 10 year old will tend to describe a friend in terms of personality and attainments, for example 'lively, fun to be with, good at swimming'. Physical characteristics are very salient for children under about 7 years old. It is what they mention when asked, in unstructured interviews, to describe other children (Livesley and Bromley, 1973). However, young children, given fixed choice questions, can refer to traits (for example, 'Is your best friend friendly, cool or hostile to other children?' will lead children to talk about, for instance, friendliness). So young children can discuss abstract characteristics but it tends not to be what they volunteer when asked about other people. It is therefore predictable that a 5 year old, when asked an open question about the special school children whom he or she had seen briefly, commented on the spectacles worn by one of those children (see earlier).

This awareness of physical cues might lead us to expect that disabilities with physical indicators (such as a wheelchair or a phonic ear) will be recognised, and understood, at an earlier age than are disabilities (such as emotional disorders) which lack physical indicators. There is much evidence to support this idea. Children as young as 5 years old have been found to classify the able bodied and physically disabled into different groups. Disordered behaviour, or maladjustment, is likely to be much less easy to recognise and understand. Some American researchers have found that 11 year olds believed maladjustment was caused by the child's environment (such as an unhappy home) but 7 year olds thought maladjustment was caused by internal, physical factors, such as an injury at birth (Maas *et al.*, 1978). An implication of this is that children under about 7 years old may have little understanding of a disability unless there is a physical sign of the disability (such as a wheelchair or spectacles).

A second change in children's knowledge of others concerns ideas about whether someone belongs to a particular group (for example, men/women, black/white, young/old, clever/silly, disabled/not disabled). Young children tend to be unequivocal about group membership. They may be certain about, for example, who is and who is not in their school class or friendship group. Research evidence suggests that by age 3 children have a rudimentary awareness of cues concerning age, sex, ethnicity and kinship (reviewed in Lewis and Lewis, 1987, 1988). So children can readily allocate people to these groups. By age 5, cues for these groups are well established.

As children move through the primary or elementary school years they begin to make more distinctions within groups – boys are noisy but not always and not all boys are noisy. Groups which are less immediately identifiable begin to be identified. For example, 'black' children are re-classified into West Indian/Asian and later children recognise sub-divisions of these groups. On this evidence we would again expect that disabled groups for whom the cues are not obvious would not be recognised as distinct groups until after around 8 years old. Some interesting work has shown that children of primary school age take what they know, in terms of abstract characteristics, about one disabled group and, if they are unsure, apply it to an unknown disabled group (Maras and Brown, 1992). This points to the importance of not over generalising about disability.

The third and related change in children's understanding about others is a knowledge of which cues about group membership do not change. For example, girls sometimes wear 'boys'' clothes but this does not change their sex; a child may dress up as an old woman but this does not change his or her real age. Researchers have found that by age 7 children recognise that gender does not change, and by age 8, that ethnic group does not change. If permanence of these relatively common groups is not fully understood until ages 7 or 8 one would not expect children younger than this to understand that disability does not change. It seems likely that understanding the permanence of less frequent or less well-recognised disabilities would occur at a much later age. One spin-off from the different ideas about the causes of maladjustment, mentioned earlier, was that the older children were much more likely than the younger children to believe that misbehaviour could be changed. This lack of recognition of the probable permanence of the disability itself may well lead children to expect disabilities to disappear as the disabled child grows up.

So developmental research points to several things to bear in mind when explaining disability to children:

- Physical disabilities are recognised and understood at a relatively young age (by about 5 years) so these can be explained simply to children above this age.
- Sensory impairments are also understood by children of around 5 years age.
- It is useful to explain to children the limited nature of the disability if they are at a stage when that disability would be understood. For example, to explain deafness as a hearing loss but nothing more; physical disability as, perhaps, a lack of mobility but nothing more.
- Emotional maladjustment is not understood by children under about age 8 or 9. Until about age 11 maladjusted behaviour tends to be seen as caused by things within the child, rather than in that child's environment. Some types of maladjustment, such as withdrawn or self-mutilating behaviour, are seen as outside the child's control. However, aggressive maladjusted behaviour is seen as wilful. Thus disabilities need to be explained objectively and without connotations of blame.
- If a child understands, or is familiar with, certain disabilities, then abstract characteristics of those disabilities will tend to be applied to people with other, less well-understood, disabilities. It is important to explain disability in terms of the specific nature of the disability and not possible effects.

Children's knowledge of disability – materials and strategies

There are various materials and strategies available to promote children's understanding of disability.

Media sources of information about the nature of disability

There is a wide range of books, magazines and other materials for professionals and parents to use to help children gain information about disability. Some of these have already been mentioned concerning preparation in relation to attitudes. Some publishers (for example, Penguin) produce specific catalogues on this theme. There are also specialist publishers in this area (for example, Barnicoats) assembling useful annotated lists of books by, or about, people with disabilities. Some informative story books concerning children with learning difficulties and aimed at different age groups were mentioned earlier. Various voluntary organisations collate related fiction and non-fiction books (for example, the National Children's Bureau runs a library and information service, for which there is a small charge for reading lists on specific topics).

Communication skills

Communication and friendship emerged as twin concerns among people who had been involved in a befriending scheme with people with learning difficulties (Richardson and Ritchie, 1989). One person said 'It is difficult for me to speak. [I] have to think about what I'm going to say before and how to approach people' (1989: 28). This underlines the importance of their co-conversationalists giving listeners time to put together a response.

There were ways in which both the mainstream and the special school pupils needed to develop some aspects of communication in order to get the most from interactions with one another. The special school pupils needed to be helped to listen attentively to mainstream school work partners, to identify the key elements in a message and to initiate conversation. Children from the mainstream school may need to develop skills in responding to the other person. This may include skills like holding back conversationally and so giving other children (here, the special school work partner) more time to reply.

Language games, alongside activities which naturally encourage pupils' attempts at communication, can help to develop these kinds of skills. (See Schiefelbusch and Pickar, 1984, and McTear and Conti-Ramsden, 1992, for a discussion of wider issues.) Games and other approaches used with pupils with learning difficulties and non-disabled young children to foster communication skills have been explored by a number of writers. (See, for example, overviews by Hutt, 1986, Locke, 1985, and Ackerman and Mount, 1991; for work associated with the National Oracy Project, see Norman, 1992; for work on developing talk in groups, see Dunne and Bennett, 1990; and for games developed with young children in mind, see Wolfendale and Bryans, 1986, and Mason and Mudd, 1993.) This is an extensive area for both research and developments in practice and the following ideas are given to illustrate a sample of possible approaches:

- Encourage eye contact, especially with the speaker, using ideas borrowed from dramatherapy (see Jennings, 1993, 1994). For example, throwing a real (for example, a bean bag) or imaginary object (for example, a 'baby dinosaur') to a child who 'catches' the object, says the name of another child and throws the object to that child.
- Build up listening skills by, for example, asking the child to identify the odd one out (by sound or meaning) in a series (for example, 'hat ham had elephant hand'; or, 'dog hat cat budgie') and giving a reason for the word chosen.
- Foster listening through 'Chinese Whispers' in which a message is passed around a group, one person whispering it to the next person.
- Develop awareness of sound and rhythm by teaching rhymes in which an adult or older child says a line and the listening child has to repeat that line.
- Promote listening and speaking through sentence-completion games in which the child is told the start of a sentence (perhaps to describe a picture) and has to complete the sentence.
- Avoid children in a group talking over one another by, for example, having a 'speaker's wand' which is held by the child speaking and passed to the next speaker.
- Share the time during which individuals in a group talk by, for example, having a 'clock watcher' who checks the length of time for which any one child in a group debate or discussion has been talking and signals when individual time (e.g. two minutes) is up.
- Share who talks by, for example, having 'chips', one per child, and when each child has spoken his or her chip is placed in the centre of the table. Nobody has a second chance to talk until everyone who wishes to has spoken once. When all chips are in the centre of the table they can be re-distributed.

These last two approaches need to be used sensitively so that quieter children do not feel uncomfortably pressurised.

PLANNING LINK SESSIONS

The activities

Each session in the Link 7 and Link 11 projects had a clear structure. It began with an opening whole group period in which the session's work was described. This was followed by a paired activity in which a child from the mainstream school and a special school pupil worked together. Each session ended with a review period in which pupils would discuss their work and (for the younger children) there were also songs and rhymes.

In both projects, sessions were planned alternately by special and mainstream school teachers. That way, it was hoped that any curricular bias towards one group or the other would be evened out. This also meant that the link sessions worked as a form of in-service education for the teachers because they were each having to plan for a group of children with a much wider range of learning needs than was usually the case for individual teachers. Teachers and the other adults involved really needed to meet between sessions to plan and review work but the practicalities meant that this had to be done by telephone rather than face to face. Sessions concentrated on art and craft activities as these could be adapted so that every child participated at an appropriate level. Both mainstream schools taught their pupils some Makaton signs (gestures to convey words and phrases such as 'hello'; used in both special schools) to help communication.

There has been considerable debate about what type of activity is most suitable for this type of project. One aspect of the debate has compared the effectiveness of structured (for example, art and craft, PE) with unstructured (for example, free play) activities in fostering interaction and positive attitudes between special and mainstream school groups. Overall, structured activities have been found more successful than were unstructured activities (Carpenter *et al.*, 1987). Perhaps this is because these involve clearly defined roles for the pupils involved and thus clarity for the children about what they are expected to do.

Within structured activities it is evident that, in early meetings, children from the mainstream school need what some writers call 'sanctioned staring', that is a time for children to look uninterruptedly at others without feeling forced into communication. This was very noticeable in a parallel to the Link 7 project in which there was little contact between special and mainstream school children for the first term of fortnightly joint sessions. Much time in these sessions was spent in children interacting with adults. There was, for mainstream school children, an unusually high proportion of adults in the classroom at this time because of the number of adults who came with the special school pupils (usually four adults). If preparatory video material is used, as suggested earlier, then the sanctioned staring phase may be countenanced through video rather than staring directly at classmates.

Various foci have been tried for shared structured activities involving pupils from special and mainstream schools working together. Successful tasks have involved art and craft, music, poetry, drama, cookery, technology, science, and physical education. The last area has been found by some researchers to be less effective than the other areas because the mainstream school culture of physical education was individualistic and non-cooperative. Physical education was seen by mainstream school children as a chance to race around letting off steam and so an obligation to work with special school work partners was felt by the mainstream school children to be constraining. Activities such as horse riding in which pupils from special schools have more experience than do mainstream school children may balance activities in which children from mainstream schools have more experience.

A central problem in the link projects was to identify tasks that required each child to make a contribution to a common activity. A repeated difficulty was in finding tasks that were:

(1) not so difficult for the special school child that he or she dropped out of the task and lost interest,
(2) not so interesting and novel for the mainstream school children that they took over the task, and
(3) not so easy for the mainstream school child that he or she lost interest.

The tasks had to fit the different skills, knowledge and attention spans of all the pupils involved. In practice, the search for complementary contributions to a common task was often replaced by tutoring of special school pupils by mainstream school children.

Nonetheless, the tasks retained an element of each child contributing. The following examples are a development of ideas familiar to teachers who plan mixed ability group work. Children had a free choice of work partners with the proviso that they must come from the other school group. The school groups within each project took it in turn to choose so that both special and mainstream school children had choices about the pupil(s) with whom they worked. Some successful tasks were as follows.

Link 7 project

- Wax resist painting in which the mainstream school child wrote or drew on the paper with a candle or clear wax crayon and the special school child painted over this.
- String painting in which the special school child put the string in paint, the mainstream school child placed it on paper and folded the paper in half, the special school child pressed the paper down.
- Potato printing in which the mainstream school child placed the potato in paint and the special school child printed with the potato piece on a sheet of paper.
- Paper bag puppets in which the mainstream school child cut out, for example, lips, hair, and the special school child glued these on.

Link 11 project

Tasks that seemed to encourage the special and mainstream school school pupils to work together included:

- joint writing, special school child dictating and mainstream school child scribing;
- joint writing using a micro-computer, children taking it in turns to compose and key in;
- puppets involving joint cutting out, gluing, discussion of result;
- rubbings in which both pupils made impressions of surfaces around the school and then collaborated on cutting out shapes from these and gluing them on to a joint collage of rubbings, labels showing where the rubbing was made written by the mainstream school child from information from both children.

Possibly the most important feature of the successful tasks was that neither pupil totally dominated the interaction. This was often difficult to achieve in practice but there is evidence from other research that tasks in which one child is always the learner, or relatively inexperienced, while the other child is invariably the skilled performer, encourage negative attitudes and limit learning in the child who is dominated (McConkey and McCormack, 1984). It is crucial that children involved in paired working all have the chance to be the teacher. The importance of this is illustrated in Joan Hebden's account of her daughter Cathy in which Cathy is shown to have valued experiences in which she could be the helper, not just the recipient of help.

> Without any prompting from us, she [Cathy] made a point of helping anyone blind, elderly or infirm to cross the road safely. The first time this happened I felt quite emotional; there was an undeniable lump in my throat when I realised that she had now become the helper, the strong one.
>
> (1985: 111)

Later Cathy was involved in a Handicapped Guides and Rangers Group: 'Even the slowest among them delights in being given special tasks to do and will beam with pleasure at the privilege of being allowed to assist anyone' (1985: 115). In the same vein Sharyn Duffin, who is blind and physically disabled, wrote, 'Would that we could structure our schools and communities to better use handicapped people as resources, to take advantage of their abilities, to give them the satisfaction inherent in helping others' (1981: 4).

Funding

Resources for the link projects were funded in two ways. In one project a central local education authority (school district) budget (distributed via the special school) covered the cost of the materials. In the other project the schools shared the costs of resources by supplying different sets of materials (for example, one school providing the paint and the other school providing paper). Issues of funding the increasing range of types of integration and the variety of arrangements encompassed by a continuum of special needs provision will not be examined here.

There have been a number of calls for resources either to follow the child and so follow him or her to wherever the child is educated (shared proportionally between placements if the child's education is split between schools). Alternatively it may be argued that if resources are allocated to schools (not to their populations specifically) each school has an incentive to spread special needs resources as it thinks most effective and not just on the 'integration child' (in Victoria, Australia, terms) or the 'statemented child' (in UK terms).

First meeting

The reception of pupils going into a special or mainstream school is an important aspect of link work. There is often much careful preparation and thought about what the pupils will do in class but they may be received into the school in an unwelcome or haphazard manner. Some schools plan welcome committees to greet children on the first couple of visits to try to ensure a good welcome. However, some schools may unwittingly overemphasise children's visitor status in apparently small ways. These may include leaving these pupils to wait in a lobby area of the school instead of going directly into classes, not providing them with routine materials, coat peg or personal drawer, leaving them out of homework arrangements, placing them on a separate register, not putting them into a school house system or in not informing their parents about types of clothing to be worn by pupils.

One of the first classroom activities that the Link 11 project pupils carried out was group writing and drawing for an entrance hall display. In pairs or threesomes (one special school with one or two mainstream school children) the pupils interviewed one another, wrote a joint piece about favourite things, and drew life-size pictures of one another. The striking aspect of this work was the speed with which the children identified things that they had in common. These included a shared enthusiasm for *Neighbours*, 'Big Macs' and puppies. These discussions served to emphasise what the pupils had in common and set the tone for the work – differences were not denied but emphasis was on similarities.

CONCLUSION

Link schemes must centre on the complementarity of special and mainstream school contexts – children, staff and schools. 'Developments' which rest on a feeling that one school is doing the other a favour are likely to be short lived.

Preparation for a link scheme requires that both special and mainstream school pupils have an understanding of each other. After the preparation and first meetings is the period of, potential, fruitful interaction. The following two chapters look at how the mainstream and special school pupils tried to communicate with one another and how they ultimately provided one another with what were probably unique social and linguistic demands.

Chapter 4

Working together
The Link 7 Project

Stephen is 8. He attends a school for children with severe learning difficulties (SLD). He works regularly with Peter, age 6, a boy from a neighbouring mainstream school. Today, they are making a puppet, together, from a paper bag. It is a typical school activity for children of this age in many countries. What is unusual here is the process of completing the activity. Peter hands Stephen some fabric eyes and mouth to glue on to the paper bag. Stephen places them on the face of the puppet, moves them around, squinting at the placing of the eyes and mouth, trying to work out the best position. Finally he nudges Peter and says 'Eh?', Peter nods, and Stephen glues the pieces into place.

Twenty-five years ago in the UK (and many other countries in the 'developed' world) children like Stephen and Peter would not have been in the same education system, let alone working together on a shared task. A child like Stephen may well have been in a hospital and thought of as needing medical not educational support. Few adults have, as children, had the sorts of experiences that have become commonplace for Stephen and Peter. We place demands on these children without having a clear idea of what these demands may involve or how the children will react. The process of communicating is exacting for both children.

Paul Williams, writing some years ago, projected what a person with learning difficulties might feel about communication with non-disabled people. He wrote:

Communication is one of our greatest areas of difficulty . . . Both of us have difficulty in communicating with, and forming relationships with, the other. . . . Problems are caused by a mutual handicap – we have difficulty in expression, you have difficulty in listening.

(1978: 2)

This chapter looks at communication between mainstream and special school children in the Link 7 project during shared activities. It draws out evidence about how, when and why communication was fostered or impeded. The findings show how pupils (from special and mainstream schools) responded to the potential barriers to communication identified by Paul Williams. All pupils had some difficulties both in getting their message across to work partners and in understanding those work partners' communication. Two pupils from the mainstream school are looked at in more detail because they provide examples of children who were enabling towards special school work partners (Hamish) or domineering (Alice). Discussion of these children includes reference to their understanding about the nature of severe learning difficulties. The implications for practice are examined further in Chapter 7.

OVERVIEW OF THE COMMUNICATION IN LINK 7 SESSIONS

Audio recordings were made of each of the ten pairs of mainstream and special school children (one child from each school type) in each of the Link 7 sessions over one school year. Throughout the year the children worked together in the same classroom for one afternoon every two weeks. The children were recorded when they were working together on a joint task, which was usually an art and craft activity. This talk may not have been typical of talk between those children in other contexts, for example when they were playing informally. The children from the mainstream school were interviewed near the beginning and at the end of the year of link sessions. Brief reference is made in this chapter to some of these views. Year-end views are discussed more fully in Chapter 6.

There has been much research and discussion about the differences between cooperation, collaboration, tutoring, helping and specific schemes such as buddy systems (see further reading on children's peer tutoring and cooperative working in classrooms). The term 'guiding' is used in this chapter although there are parallels with children's tutoring of other children. Focus here is on novice guide and partner roles because these were the main roles taken by the mainstream and special school children, respectively, during the shared activities. 'Novice guide', rather than 'tutor', is used as the context was not explicitly directive; emphasis was on collaborating, not teaching a specific skill. 'Novice' emphasises the novelty of the situation and that it was an untried forum in which to exercise guidance. The mainstream school children were preoccupied with trying to encourage the special school children to complete their parts in the joint tasks and the mainstream school children often reiterated adults' instructions that the children should work together on the tasks. The special school pupil's role is described as that of a 'partner', not a 'tutee', to avoid unwarranted connotations of passivity and lower status.

One comparison session was held with these same mainstream school children working with younger children (4 and 5 year olds) from the mainstream school. Those children knew one another by sight but had not worked together before. The kinds of activities in which the children engaged were similar to those of the 6 and 7 year olds working with special school work partners. The comparison session with younger mainstream school children was held at the end of the year. It will be mentioned only briefly here but it did provide some interesting parallels with talk between special and mainstream school pupils. These comparisons are reported when they are relevant to the discussion of interactions in the Link 7 sessions. (See Lewis, 1990, for more analyses and discussion of these comparisons.)

Predictably, the 6 and 7 year old mainstream school children dominated the talk with special school work partners. The mainstream school children said nine times as much as did the special school children. In fact in a whole year of audio recordings of talk between mainstream and special school children, while they were working together on shared tasks, there were 2200 comments by mainstream school children but only 240 comments by special school children. This compares with about 1000 comments by these mainstream school children in one session working with younger mainstream school children. These younger children said less (about 400 comments in total) than did the older children. So in both contexts the 6 and 7 year old mainstream school children dominated conversation and this was particularly marked when they worked with special school work partners.

The mainstream school children also spoke for longer than did the special school children. These children rarely gave more than single word comments and much of their speech comprised vocalisations which could not be interpreted by other children or most of the adults present. Observation notes made during the link sessions show that the special school children were tending to communicate non-verbally (for example, using Makaton signs). However, because only audio recordings were made there were no analyses of this non-verbal interaction. The emphasis in this chapter is on talk and therefore the mainstream school children feature strongly. However, non-verbal behaviour by children from the special school is explored later in this chapter in descriptive accounts of occasions when there was tension between work partners.

CHILDREN'S DEVELOPMENT AS TUTORS TO OTHER CHILDREN

Children as young as 2½ years old are able to act as a teacher to another child (see further reading on language development). However, although, at this age, child tutors are able to give instructions and to demonstrate a task, they often give inadequate instructions. They also fail to give the learner feedback about whether he or she is succeeding on the task. So child tutors of this age can convey simple task instructions but are insufficiently responsive to learners to be very effective teachers. Effective tutoring requires the tutor to assess many things concurrently. These include the various demands of the task, the needs of the learner and the interaction of these two sets of factors. A child teaching another child, for example, to cut out a circle, has to know how to cut out circles (including the related language like 'scissors', 'cut', 'down', 'round'), have the manipulative skills to demonstrate cutting out, if necessary, and have the social skills to know when to give what types of instruction, encouragement and so on. The child tutor has to be sufficiently flexible to keep monitoring these and changing tactics as needed.

Work by David Wood and his co-workers into the tutoring skills of 3, 5 and 7 year olds has shown that 3 and 5 year olds tend to make unskilled tutors (Wood, 1993). At age 7 children begin to be able to stand back from the task and be more flexible. For example, they begin to accept unusual but correct ways of completing a problem. Also, they will give a prompt and then let the learner complete the task independently. This work is particularly interesting because earlier research had indicated that children would not really stand back from a task until around ages 10 or 11. The difference is important here because of the implications for whether young children will make effective tutors of children with learning difficulties.

Lynn Fuchs and her co-researchers (Fuchs *et al.*, 1994) have reported research concerning the effects of previous training and experience in peer tutoring on a mathematics task with 9 to 11 year olds. Their work indicates that inexperienced tutors, slightly older than the children involved in this link project, provided little opportunity for tutees to apply or practise the tutor's instructions or demonstrations. In other words, they were not displaying the self-inhibition found by David Wood with some 7 year olds. However, Lynn Fuchs and her colleagues found that experience in peer tutoring made a difference. Experienced child tutors, compared with the inexperienced, structured more interactions, guided tutees to rehearse the necessary steps and actively involved tutees.

One aspect of tutoring is the way in which instructions, feedback and other comments are phrased. Children, until they are about 4 years old (in terms of either chronological age or maturity), tend to phrase things in ways which are dominated by the wish to give a particular message. They do not think so much about what is appropriate in that context. So a young child who is hungry when it is not a mealtime says that he or she wants a sandwich; if the child dislikes someone and wants them to go away then he or she will say so directly. However, quite early, even as young as 2 years old, children start to recognise that directness is not always the best policy. Sometimes more polite forms are more acceptable and more effective. 'Can I have a sandwich please?' is often conspicuously more successful than 'I want a sandwich.' 'We could have a sandwich now' is even less direct but carries the same message. The more that the child is aware, albeit sub-consciously, of social nuances, the more he or she will use a range of phrasings, choosing the phrasing that seems to fit the situation. So we can infer something about the child's understanding of the situation from his or her phrasing.

The situation includes the listener and the relationship between the child and his or her listener. We know, from a range of research evidence, that from about 5 years old children start to adjust what they say depending on the characteristics of the listener (Shatz and Gelman, 1973; Garvey, 1984). They do not talk to every listener in the same way, even if what they want to convey is basically the same message. Familiarity, age, status and attainments of the listener have all been shown to influence how children phrase their messages. For example, a 5 year old talking to a 3, 11 and 18 year old phrases things differently for the various listeners even if the intention (for example, 'I want a sandwich') is the same in each case. Many factors are interacting here such as how well the child knows the listener, how well they get on, what their respective roles are, what the activity is, and so on.

There is a cluster of characteristics that research in many contexts and various countries has found to typify children's talk to children who are younger than themselves or who are thought of as being of lower status. Joyce Grenfell's caricature of a nursery teacher illustrates many of these features. Comments are repeated frequently and there are many instructions to do, or desist from, something. These instructions are phrased in a very direct way. There are few explanations and few genuine questions. This cluster of characteristics recurs in children's talk to dolls, to younger children, to children for whom English is a second language, to children with learning difficulties and to submissive children.

This work points to several things that we might expect of the Link 7 mainstream school children (who were 6 and 7 years old) when working with children from the special school. We would expect the mainstream school children to be quite effective guides. They would probably be polite and indirect if they saw the situation as requiring this but they would tend to use a dominant style to special school work partners. It is clear from scrutinising the flow of the interaction, as revealed through the children's talk, that these things did happen.

TALK IN LINK 7 SESSIONS

Mainstream school children's talk to special school work partners while working on shared tasks can be summed up as 'bossy'. This is shown in Figure 13 which classifies the comments of mainstream school children to special school work partners during the shared activity part of link sessions over one school year. (Results for sessions across the year are grouped because statistical analyses showed that there were no systematic differences across sessions, or for different mainstream school children, or for different special school work partners; see Lewis, 1990.) The 'bossy' label may be unfair to the mainstream school children. They did show sensitivity to what they thought to be the special school children's

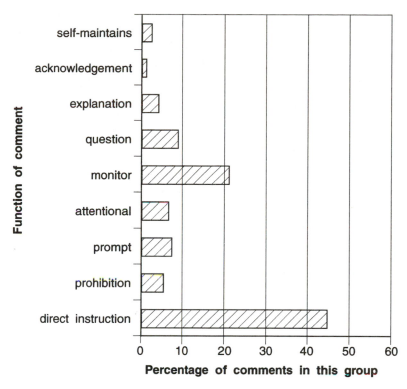

Figure 13 Link 7 project: talk by children in the mainstream school to work partners from the special school

Notes: Key to graph:

direct instruction: an explicit command or request to do something, e.g. 'sit down'
prohibition: an instruction not to do something e.g. 'don't do that'
prompt: a hint about a course of action e.g. 'you could do it there'
attentional: a call to get the attention of the listener e.g. 'hey'
monitor: describing/commenting on what is happening e.g. 'it's going red now'
question: comments which involved the listener making a choice e.g. 'which one now?'
explanation: explaining a point or giving a reason e.g. 'we've got to do pink because . . .'
acknowledgement: recognising the listener's comment or gesture e.g. 'OK'
self-maintains: defending own position e.g. 'get off, that's mine'.

Source: Adapted from Dore (1986).
Comments could be coded more than once; categories were not mutually exclusive.

learning needs and were probably not explicitly setting out to dominate the interaction.

We know from a wide range of classroom research that teachers tend to be very directive when talking to children and that the more directive teachers are, the less children initiate conversation (Conti-Ramsden and Taylor, 1990). So the mainstream school children may, to some extent, have been copying the ways in which teachers had talked to pupils.

Mainstream school pupils' attempts to guide special school pupils through a task is now discussed under headings relating to the various elements embodied in cooperating on a task. These headings have been extrapolated from analyses of guiding in the the link projects and from findings in the research literature into peer tutoring (see further reading on children's peer tutoring and cooperative working in classrooms). The key aspects are:

(1) getting the attention of the partner
(2) keeping the attention of the partner
(3) preparing for the task
(4) organising the task in a relevant way
(5) identifying the partner's learning needs
(6) monitoring the partner's apparent successes and failures
(7) holding back from completing the task oneself
(8) demonstrating and explaining the task
(9) integrating these activities and sets of information.

These elements will not necessarily take place in this sequence. For example, a child acting as a guide might decide to begin by demonstrating the task and not wait for the partner to make possible errors. The various elements interact but are discussed here individually. This shows the ways in which mainstream school children used each of these strategies when working with children from the special school.

Getting the attention of the partner

No guiding can be effective if the partner is not attending to, and interested in, the task. So the first job of a guide is to get the partner hooked on the task. Strategies to obtain the partner's attention include:

- using the child's name ('Hey Jasmine!'),
- an expression that will get the listener's attention ('Wow! Look at this!'),
- display questions ('It's good, isn't it?'),
- genuine questions ('Do you want to do this?'),
- a tone, probably relatively high pitched, that is 'ear-catching',
- making eye contact,
- pointing to the object of the talk,
- touching the partner, and/or
- making a gesture that draws the other child into the task, for example turning a doll over so that it cries, or placing objects in a half-completed position.

Research findings indicate that young children (3 to 5 years) use these kinds of features more frequently when interacting with younger children than they do when communicating with older children or adults. Even young children use these kinds of strategies to get inattentive listeners to attend. Whether this applies to young children with learning difficulties when they are guides to other children is not clear. There is little research about this.

Many of the children from the mainstream school talked in interviews about concerns in controlling children from the special school (see Chapter 6). Consequently, one might expect that securing those children's attention would be a high priority. Indeed, much (nearly one-tenth) of all mainstream school children's talk to special school work partners was in the form of one of the attention-getting strategies described earlier. In particular, mainstream school children used an exclamation with the partner's name (e.g. 'Hey Michael!', 'Wowee Frankie!', shown as attentionals in Figure 13).

This occurred frequently with individual special school children (particularly David) whom virtually all the mainstream school children found inattentive. The mainstream school children had a limited range of strategies to bring special school children back to the task. They were often at a loss about how to respond to inattentivity, beyond repeating the child's name, using an increasingly firm tone of voice and repeating instructions. The following extract is unusual in that Andrew (age 6, from the mainstream school) used a relatively wide range of strategies to secure David's (age 6, from the special school) attention while painting. (The interaction was accompanied by observation notes but was not video taped, so it is not possible to assess the detailed non-verbal techniques that the children may have been using.) (Transcription conventions are given on page xi).

Andrew:	Hey!
	[calling to get David's attention]
David:	(no response)
Andrew:	*Take* it!
David:	(no response)
Andrew:	*Take* it!
	[instruction repeated]
David:	(no response)
Andrew:	Shall we just do
David:	(no response)
Andrew:	Paint it
David:	(no response)
Andrew:	Paint
	[instruction re-phrased]
David:	(loud vocalisation)
	[not interpretable]
Andrew:	OK
	OK
	Look David
	[instruction + David's name]
David:	(no response)
Andrew:	D'you want to paint over it now?
	[instruction in question form]
David:	(no response)
Andrew:	*David*, d'you want to paint it?
	[name + re-phrased question]
David:	(no response)
Andrew:	**DAVID!**
	David
	David
	David
	((handing David brush))
	Now do some painting *over* it
	Do some painting
	[re-phrased instruction]
	Now put paint over it David
	[re-phrased instruction]
David:	(no response)

Andrew: I'll help you
                [involving self]
                I'll show you
                ((showing task))
                [demonstrating]
                This is it
                I'll show you

This episode lasted for three minutes. Andrew tried a range of strategies to engage David, a child whose attention the teachers also had difficulty in holding. Andrew tried direct instructions, an instruction disguised as a question, using David's name and demonstrating. Andrew rarely repeated a failed instruction and was persistent in trying to find other ways in which to put his message across. David's lack of cooperation seems to have prompted Andrew to draw on a wide range of attention-getting strategies. None of these were required, and so were not demonstrated, in Andrew's interactions with his more compliant work partners (from either the special school or the younger mainstream school class). So talk with special school work partners was either developing these strategies and/or allowing them to be aired.

Keeping the attention and interest of the partner

Once attention had been secured then the child acting as a guide had to sustain interest and attention on the task. Nearly one-quarter of the talk by mainstream school children to special school work partners was in the form of monitoring, or describing, what was happening (for example, 'The paint's going orangey'; 'This bit's getting tricky') (see Figure 13). When these same mainstream school children carried out similar activities with 4 and 5 year olds from the mainstream school this monitoring category of talk was even higher (nearly 50 per cent) of all the 6 and 7 year olds' talk to the younger children. Arguably, this type of running commentary is an effective, although low key, way of sustaining the listener's interest and attention. It is less overt than Andrew's strategies to David but acts as a continual reminder of the task to the partner and reminds the partner of the guide's interest and attention. Interestingly, a training package for parents of non-compliant children (Forehand and McMahon, 1981) emphasised a similar point. Their 'Child's Game', which has been evaluated extensively in both home and laboratory trials, involves training parents to give 'attends' (commentaries on the child's actions) to show that they are interested in the child's activity.

A less subtle way to keep the listener involved is to give him or her instructions. This demands some involvement. All except one of the Link 7 mainstream school children routinely began a sequence of instructions to their work partners with an indirect instruction. For example:

'Would you like to . . .'

'We could . . .'

'How about . . .'

'It might be a good idea to . . .'

If and when this failed, the guides moved on to phrasing the instruction more directly, if necessary repeating or changing this slightly until the special school work partner understood. This is illustrated in Michelle's (age 6, from the mainstream school) talk to Lucy (age 6, from the special school). Michelle and Lucy were making a collage of a woman.

Michelle: You could put the dress there
Lucy: (no response)
Michelle: Do you want to put the dress there?
Lucy: (no response)
Michelle: Put the dress there
Lucy: ((glues dress on paper as indicated by Michelle))

Michelle began with a prompt about what Lucy should do in the task. Michelle did not begin, apparently, with the idea that 'This child is very stupid, I'll have to spell out exactly what she must do' but rather said the same kind of thing to Lucy that she said to younger children when working with them on similar tasks. However, this hint about what to do ('You could put the dress there') did not lead Lucy to respond so Michelle was forced to reconsider her instruction. She did not just repeat this instruction which had already failed to draw out the right response. Michelle changed her prompt into something slightly more direct, a question used as an instruction ('Do you want to put the dress there?'). This, potentially, required greater involvement from Lucy because by being phrased as a question it invited a response. Only when Lucy still did not respond, did Michelle turn the question into a direct instruction ('Put the dress there'). This sequence shows in microcosm the sort of process which was repeated regularly when these mainstream and special school children worked together. A prompt tended to be followed with a series of direct instructions. Consequently, there was a relatively low proportion of prompts overall in these mainstream school 7 year olds' talk to special school work partners (see Figure 13).

Nearly half of all the speech by Link 7 mainstream school children to special school work partners was in the form of direct instructions, such as 'Colour it in there' or 'You pick it up' (see Figure 13). This represented a much higher proportion of direct instructions than was found when these same mainstream school children worked on similar tasks with mainstream school 4 and 5 year olds. Less than a quarter of all talk to these younger children was of this highly directive type. So it seems that these 6 and 7 year old mainstream school children were probably making adjustments to special school work partners. One of these adjustments was along the lines of 'I'll have to say this more clearly and directly'. This was most noticeable in the re-phrasing of comments from indirect to successively more direct forms. Intuitively these mainstream school children often addressed special school work partners in ways likely to help them through the task without being too directive.

Perhaps the easiest way to keep the attention of a partner was just to repeat something if it had not generated the right, or any, response. There was a very high proportion of repeated comments in the talk of the mainstream school children to special school work partners. Overall, over one-tenth of all their comments were a direct repeat of something they had just said. By comparison, repeated comments were half as frequent as this in those same children's talk to mainstream school 4 and 5 year olds. There are various possible reasons underlying the relatively high use of repetitions by mainstream school children when addressing special school partners. These reasons include the presumed hearing impairments of special school pupils which may have led mainstream school children to repeat comments (see Chapter 6). Frequently repeating a comment may also have been the result of how special school children reacted. There is evidence that 3 and 4 year olds tend to be impulsive listeners. They tend to focus on what are thought to be key elements in the speaker's instruction at too early a point in the communication. If this was happening with special school partners making hasty non-verbal responses then this may also have prompted mainstream school children to repeat, rather than to re-phrase, an utterance.

Simply repeating a comment was often ineffective in getting the message across to the special school work partner, as is illustrated in Hamish's talk with Ben when Hamish had taken Ben to the washroom to wipe his face:

Hamish:	*Don't* put it in your mouth
	Don't put it in your mouth
	Wash your face with that
	Wash it
	Then wipe it round
	Wash it
Ben:	((washing face with cloth?))
Hamish:	That's it
	Don't put it in your mouth
	Don't put it in your mouth
	Wash your face now
	Wash your face now
	Wash your face now
	Your face, wash it this side
	Yeh

Ben seemed to act on Hamish's instruction when it had been re-phrased, rather than when it had only been repeated in the original form. It may be that Ben just needed more time in which to make a response and whether the action followed a repeat or a re-phrasing was irrelevant. It may be useful explicitly to encourage children in this situation to give the other child plenty of time to respond.

Preparing for the task

When the partner's attention had been obtained then the child acting as a guide focused on the demands of the task. Mainstream school children began a sequence of instruction in a very logical way by orienting their special school work partners to the specific task:

'Next we're going to do the eyes' (Steve)

'We've got to try and make a little boy' (Ruth)

'I'll spread them about . . . put it together to make a square . . . see if you can' (Hamish)

'I'll draw round it once and in another place you're going to draw round it' (Alice)

'We're going to do the little gingerbread boy, aren't we?' (Rachel)

'We're making a duck ain't we?' (Andrew)

There were similar, although less frequent, examples in the comparison session involving mainstream school children guiding 4 and 5 year olds from the mainstream school, for example:

'I know what to draw. Draw a road with all cars on' (Liam)

Again, this shows an intuitively helpful way of starting instructions although the special school work partners were a novel group for the mainstream school children with whom they worked.

Organising the task in a relevant way

The guide, having framed the task initially, then had to guide the partner through the activity. This often involved breaking the task down into small steps. Mainstream school children also drew attention to the things likely to be most useful. For example, when making a jigsaw, it is usually more useful to begin by looking at edge shapes and then to look for picture clues, not the other way round. There were many examples of mainstream school children breaking down tasks into sequences of logical small steps for special school work partners. It may be the case that the guiding of children from the special schools reinforced a step by step teaching style in the mainstream school children. It has been suggested that this is an ineffective teaching style for some areas of learning (for example, problem solving). It would be interesting to know what effect, if any, early experience of a step by step style has on peer tutoring in other contexts.

This sub-dividing of a task was illustrated in Ruth's strategies when encouraging Melanie to start painting:

Ruth: Put your dip in the paint
           Then paint it all over
           Paint all over
           All there

This illustrates what some cognitive psychologists have referred to as the tutor's ability to adjust 'grain size of instruction' to learning. It is clearly a very fundamental aspect of effective tutoring.

Identifying the partner's learning needs

Earlier, work showing that, as tutors, children address older or younger tutees in different ways was summarised. To what extent do children make fine-grained adjustments to work partners? The extent to which children seem to be identifying, and taking into account, listener needs can be examined in two ways. First, it may be done indirectly, by making inferences from group studies of children's talk to different sets of listeners. Arguably we can, if the same speakers are involved and the situations are similar, infer that differences in speech styles reflect something to do with the listener. This has been the reasoning behind a range of work that has looked, in particular, at how children talk to listeners with visual impairments, hearing impairments or varying degrees of learning difficulties.

Researchers (for example, Guralnick, 1990; Guralnick and Paul-Brown, 1980, 1984, 1989) have compared individual children's talk with non-disabled children and to classmates with mild, moderate or severe learning difficulties. They found that talk to children with moderate or severe learning difficulties was less complex, less frequent, less diverse and more directive than was speech to non-disabled children or to children with mild learning difficulties. Most of these studies tell us little about the direct influence of the children with learning difficulties because we have no information about what they were saying or doing. So it is not clear what it was about the listener that prompted the use of particular strategies. Studies investigating the contributions of young children with learning difficulties in conversations with non-disabled classmates suggest that the children with learning difficulties tended to have less influence than the non-disabled in directing the course of the task. This topic is considered more fully in the following chapter in which talk between 12 to 15 year olds with severe learning difficulties and non-disabled classmates is discussed.

It seems that in general, non-disabled children as young as 5 do make some adjustments to the apparent needs of broadly different listeners although it is not clear how finely tuned are these adjustments. However, young children often fail to make these adjustments because they do not realise that the listener has not understood the message (Light, 1987). In order to explore these points, researchers have moved to a more direct way of examining adjustment to the listener, that is by examining the flow of short sequences of talk (as in this chapter). The researcher, by examining the ebb and flow of the talk, can try to judge how sensitively one child is responding to another.

Talk by the mainstream school 6 and 7 year olds to special school work partners suggested that the mainstream school children had high expectations of those children. This was reflected in the children from the mainstream school beginning with an instruction which was phrased in an indirect way. These mainstream school children began instructions to special school work partners at a relatively complex level and only changed these into more direct and simpler forms when no response was forthcoming. This reflects two important elements: high initial expectations coupled with sensitivity to failed messages. High expectations are also indicated by the vocabulary used. These mainstream school 6 and 7 year olds used words to special school work partners like 'circle', 'pair' and 'around' which were likely to have been outside those children's vocabulary. The mainstream school children simplified these words when they seemed not to have been understood. Beginning at a relatively high level in this way is likely to be a helpful strategy because it does not underestimate the listener but at the same time the succeeding simplification makes success on the task more likely. Barbara Rogoff (1990) makes the interesting point that more sensitivity is not necessarily better. She suggests that variation in the sensitivity of support may be necessary for children to stretch their understanding and skills. In the context of the Link 7 project, some insensitivity to special school partners' learning needs may have led to comparatively high level, and hence more demanding, instructions to them.

The most obvious way to identify partners' needs is to ask them questions. Only 8 per cent of these mainstream school children's comments to special school work partners were questions (see

Figure 13). Questions were twice as frequent in talk to younger mainstream school work partners. (Questions formed 15 per cent of talk there when working on common tasks.)

There was also a difference in the type of questions asked in the two contexts. Questions to special school work partners were virtually all (nearly 90 per cent) closed questions requiring a 'yes' or 'no' answer, or a choice between two alternatives (for example, 'D'you want green paint or yellow?'). However, with the younger mainstream school children, questions were divided approximately equally between closed and open questions (i.e. questions which could have been answered in a wide range of ways). Although the use of closed questions is more restricting, it was appropriate given the limited spoken language of most of the special school work partners; they could respond non-verbally to many closed questions.

Monitoring the partner's apparent successes and failures

The child guide has to secure the partner's attention, formulate a plan about how to carry out the task and also provide the partner with some direct feedback on how he or she is doing on the task. The mainstream school children gave little explicit feedback to their work partners. The feedback that they did give concerned behaviour as well as the task. Invariably, explicit verbal feedback concerned behaviour initially and later the task. Feedback statements by mainstream school children addressing special school children included:

'That's nice, isn't it?' (Rachel)

'You're a good writer' (Liam)

'Don't do that yet' (Andrew)

'This one's all right' (Hamish)

'Watch me. Good girl' (Samantha)

'That's the wrong way . . . That's right' (Michelle)

'Like that . . . Not like that' (Carl)

'Need to press a bit harder, I think' (Samantha)

'You're putting too much paint' (Alice)

These comments are representative of feedback in Link 7 sessions over the year. There were both positive and negative comments although positive outweighed negative feedback. Feedback about behaviour tended to be very general (for example, 'Good boy') with no reference to what it was specifically about the behaviour that was deemed 'good' or 'bad'. Task-related feedback also tended to be general but there were examples, as in the last two above, in which the partner was given explicit feedback about a particular aspect of the task. This specific feedback is likely to have been more helpful to the partner than general positive comments because focused feedback pinpointed exactly what needed to be changed or had been done well.

Providing feedback is a relatively obvious way for the guide to show that he or she is monitoring the partner's successes and failures. It is less obvious that what the guide says or does when a message seems not to have been understood by the partner is also a vital part of monitoring responses (or lack of them). There is a high proportion of unsuccessful messages in young children's talk. One researcher found that approximately one-sixth of talk between pairs of $3\frac{1}{2}$ to 5 year olds comprised failed communications (Mueller, 1972). Similarly approximately one-fifth of comments by 4 and 5 year olds, who were working in pairs on a relatively simple task, were 'failed' messages. This proportion increased to nearly half when the task was more difficult (Lloyd, 1982). This suggests that young children often receive no response when they are trying to communicate with other children. Whom do children see as responsible for this lack of communication – the speaker or the listener?

Five year olds assume that as long as the message given is consistent with the intended meaning then the message is adequate. The 'fault' must lie with the listener. Similarly, research into how children tell others how to get from one place to another shows that up to the age of 7, children tend to blame the listener if a message is not understood. They seem to be unaware that the speaker's message may be inadequate and so the root of miscommunication. The mainstream school children who believed that the special school children were deaf (see Chapter 6) may have been using this as a way of attributing the cause of unsuccessful communication to the listener.

What children do when a message does not succeed is important. Does the speaker merely repeat what has just been said? Does he or she try to change the wording and/or use a non-verbal gesture? Talk by mainstream school children in the Link 7 project often met with no response or an inappropriate response (such as saying 'yes' when asked 'What colour is this?'). If mainstream school children were alert to failed messages then one would expect to find that they used strategies to try to repair the failed communication. This occurred extensively. Overall, over 10 per cent of comments by mainstream school children to special school children were re-phrasings of earlier comments in the same segment of conversation. This was a very similar proportion to the repeating of comments within the same segment of conversation, mentioned earlier. Re-phrasing was much more frequent than when those same mainstream school children talked to 4 and 5 year old mainstream school children. So for some reason, special school children received many re-phrasings. This may have been to do with the ways in which the special school children acted and/or what the mainstream school children believed about their special school work partners. Taken together, nearly a quarter of all talk by mainstream school children to their work partners from the special school was a repeat or a re-phrasing. This suggests a high degree of persistence in keeping the conversation going.

The overall figures mask wide variations between individual mainstream school children in their usage of re-phrasing or repeating of comments to special school work partners during the year. This variability is shown in Figures 14 and 15.

Repetition and re-phrasing refer to comments within a speech topic. For example, a child might say 'Cut out a circle now' (i.e. to make a wheel), when making a picture of a car, and the other child would do so. Then the instruction might be given again in the same or slightly different form (to make a second wheel) but this would not count as a repetition or rephrasing within the speech topic because the comment had a new focus. Repetitions and re-phrasings only counted as such when those comments clearly referred to one immediate task or one focus in the conversation. The vertical lines in Figures 14 and 15 show the range, from the lowest to the highest percentage of repetitions and re-phrasings, in sessions during the year of the link project. For example, Andrew's repetitions ranged from 3.6 per cent of his comments to his special school work partner in one session to 38.9 per cent of his comments in another session. On average (i.e. the mean) just over one-fifth (21.5 per cent) of his comments in all sessions were a repetition.

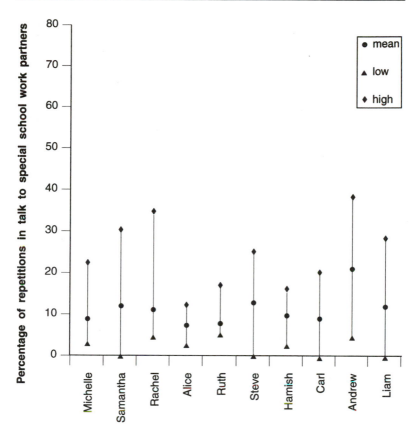

Figure 14 Link 7 project: repetitions in talk by children from the mainstream school to work partners from the special school

Figures 14 and 15 can be considered from three different perspectives: use of repeats and re-phrasing overall, use by individual children of one strategy rather than the other, and whether this varied much between sessions. Looking at these patterns helps to identify children who were enabling in their style of interaction with work partners from the special school in contrast to children who were comparatively limiting. Some children, notably Andrew and to a lesser extent Hamish, used both repeating and re-phrasing strategies a lot while Alice used them comparatively little. The former suggests a strong attempt to communicate but perhaps also

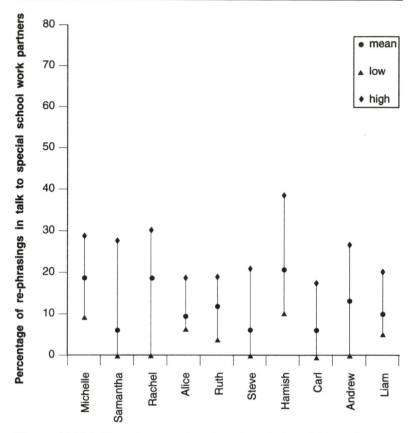

Figure 15 Link 7 project: re-phrasings in talk by children from the mainstream school to work partners from the special school

inappropriate starting points for instructions. Conversely, Alice's infrequent use of repeating and re-phrasing may have arisen because communication was successful at the outset or because she did not persist in trying to get a message across.

If Figures 14 and 15 are compared, it can be seen that some children (like Hamish) tended to re-phrase rather than to repeat comments. Arguably, successively re-phrasing a failed message was more appropriate than repeating it. Steve is an example of a child who repeated comments more frequently than he re-phrased comments. We do not know why children used the strategies that they did; it may have related to what they understood about the nature of severe learning difficulties. For example, Steve was one of the children who described the special school children generally as having hearing impairments. So for him repeating comments may have seemed a logical and appropriate response to failed attempts to communicate. If this speculative association is correct then it illustrates the importance of the messages given to children about the nature of disability.

The vertical lines in Figures 14 and 15 give an indication of the range between sessions in the use of repetitions and re-phrasings. Some children, notably Alice, were relatively consistent. The range of repeating and re-phrasing was narrower for Alice than it was for other children from the mainstream school, suggesting perhaps that she was responding stereotypically to special school work partners. As a whole, there was no consistent pattern in the use by the group of mainstream school children in their repeating or re-phrasing of comments to particular special school children. It was not the case, for example, that David, whom all the mainstream school children found very inattentive, received many repetitions of comments from all mainstream school work partners. Similarly, there were no statistically significant patterns across sessions. It was not the case, for example, that all children tended to begin with few repetitions and to increase these over the year of the link sessions.

Figures 14 and 15 do not show sequences of repeating or re-phrasing. For example, re-phrasing something, getting no response, moving to a new topic, then again re-phrasing suggests a different style of interaction from that in which many re-phrasings are made within one topic of conversation (see Lewis, 1990, for further discussion of this topic). So it is interesting to look at strings of repeating and re-phrasing and to see how these differed between children. Hamish and Michelle successively re-phrased their comments much more frequently than did the other mainstream school children. Andrew and Steve successively repeated comments more frequently.

Types of re-phrasing

The types of re-phrasing made by mainstream school children are interesting. They provide clues about the elements of the comment which were perceived as creating difficulties for work partners. For example, Steve's re-phrasings in the following extract did little to help his partner, Pip, to understand the message:

Steve: Here ((pointing))
           Paint here
           Here
           There
           DO IT HERE
           DO IT HERE
           Do it

Other mainstream school children were more effective in judging the types of re-phrasing needed for successful communication:

Michelle: Emily, d'you want to do another colour?
              Want to do another colour?
              Right we'll do this colour
              Shall we do this?
              Shall we?

In each of these successive comments Michelle re-phrased the instruction slightly. She dropped words that seemed redundant and switched between questions and 'declarative' statements. In four successive re-phrasings the comment decreased from nine to two morphemes. (A morpheme is a minimum unit of meaning; for example, 'speaking' contains two morphemes – 'speak' (the action) and 'ing' (the present tense).) This cutting down of what was said retained the most crucial elements for the communication. This gave Emily correspondingly less material to memorise and interpret before responding. Interestingly, Michelle used 'we', not 'I' or 'you', perhaps suggesting that she had understood the teachers' emphasis on the task being carried out jointly.

Four types of re-phrasing were most common. These occurred across all the mainstream school children. One type of re-phrasing was to reduce the length of the comment (as in Michelle's talk to Emily, above). Another type of re-phrasing was to change the deictic terms. These are words, such as 'it', 'that' and 'her', which point to something unspecified. These terms were often changed to the appropriate noun or noun phrase, for example changing

'Colour in *that*' to

'Colour in *the circle*'

A third kind of re-phrasing was to change the vocabulary and substitute words likely to be more familiar to the partner. An example of this was changing

'Colour in the *circle*' to

'Colour in the *round*'

Another common form of re-phrasing was to give successively more direct forms of instruction, for example changing

'You *could* put it there' to

'Put it there'

There were very few examples of re-phrasing which made the comment more complex in terms of the syntax and/or vocabulary. A hypothetical (and extreme) example of this would be changing

'Put the round next to the triangle' to

'Locate the circle alongside the scalene'

There is a trade-off between making a comment simpler to understand and making it less specific.

Despite the many examples of appropriate re-phrasing of comments, mainstream school children occasionally used terms which were probably not understood by special school partners. Yet the mainstream school children did not re-phrase these, for example:

'Can you do a *triangle* for the legs?' (Alice)

'You're doing a *tractor*' (Alice)

'Try a different *surface*?' (Ruth)

It seems that these comments were not followed with a re-phrasing because the partner made some form of response. This was often a nod or 'yes' and so the partner did not draw the guide's attention to any lack of understanding (if indeed the word was not known).

We need to bear in mind several points when examining whether these mainstream school children appeared to identify, and to act on, what they thought were the needs of their partners. The mainstream school children, although they recognised that partners needed different sorts of information from that given, still may not have acted on this understanding. The mainstream school children, if they recognised that a message had not been understood, may also have blamed their partners rather than the way in which the message had been phrased, and so did not re-phrase the message. Finally, we cannot know to what cues mainstream school children were responding. It was not necessarily attainment or developmental cues but could have been presumed hearing loss, behaviour, familiarity, or apparent chronological age which led a child from the mainstream school to repeat or re-phrase a comment.

Holding back from completing the task oneself

Work by David Wood and his co-workers is showing that it is important for the guide to stand back from a task if the partner is to have the chance to try, perhaps make mistakes and, eventually, to succeed in the task (Wood, 1993). This standing back ('self-inhibition') was rare among these mainstream school children working with special school children. Instead, when special school work partners seemed to be encountering problems the mainstream school children tended to leap in and complete the task. This is not to say that the mainstream school children were unable to stand back from the task. Rather, the context may have discouraged them from doing so because mainstream school children may have felt that teachers expected them overtly to help special school work partners. Interestingly, however, on one recorded occasion a child from the mainstream school deliberately refrained from taking over a joint task and turned to a nearby adult saying, 'He can do it really'.

Demonstrating and explaining the task

The mainstream school children gave few explanations to special school work partners. About 3 per cent of all talk to these children could be described as giving an explanation (see Figure 13). This was also unusual, although slightly more frequent, in talk to mainstream school 4 and 5 year olds. The lack of explanations limited the generalisability of what was being said. For example, an instruction to 'Cut the wheel in a circle to make it go round OK' includes information about resistance – the circular shape will rotate more easily than irregular shapes. The instruction 'Cut it round' is less useful because it lacks the general explanation.

Demonstrating was very infrequent. The extract from Andrew's talk to David, given earlier in this chapter, included modelling a correct response. One reason for the few examples of demonstrating may be the emphasis on audio data. However, observational notes were made throughout the Link 7 sessions and few mainstream school children were seen demonstrating the task for their partner. This may have reflected their difficulties in holding back from the task.

Integrating these activities and sets of information: Hamish

By age 7 the mainstream school children had mastered the basics of guiding a work partner through a task. They understood broadly what the roles of guide and partner involved. They also recognised that the guide must obtain the partner's attention, orient the partner to the task's nature and procedures, break the task down into small steps, provide encouragement and feedback and try to draw out correct responses. The mainstream school children seemed to have strong linear models of how to complete the tasks and tried to keep to these. They were inflexible about allowing the partner to deviate from this sequence and so continually tried to pull the partner back to this chain. The mainstream school children seemed to adopt the adults' rules about the task, or the context, and were persistent about trying to keep to these rules. The concept of guide held by these mainstream school children seems to have been a very didactic one. It was not, for example, of a friend who is subtly enabling, shares information and lets the partner share the lead. It would be interesting to know more about the children's concept of the teacher role as the large majority of research into children's peer tutoring reflects this same, very didactic, model.

Hamish is now discussed in more detail because his interactions reflect an enabling style with his work partners. Hamish was a quiet child whom his teacher described as slightly above average attainments compared with classmates. Hamish had one brother who was four years older than himself. Hamish was just 6 at the start of the link sessions and had had no previous contact with people with disabilities or children attending special schools. When interviewed near the start of the Link 7 project he had (wrongly) assumed that the classmates in the mainstream school whom he described as having difficulties with their work were the younger children in the class. In other words he made an assumption that low attainments were associated with young age.

Hamish talked with me after two link sessions about the children from the special school. He described these children in terms of 'things wrong with them' which he interpreted as physical disabilities – presumed inabilities to hear, talk, see correctly or walk easily. He estimated those children to be around 6 or 7 years old. This guess was close to their actual ages; these ranged from 4 to 8 years. He thought these children needed a lot of help, especially with writing which Hamish thought they found boring. He identified one child from the special school (Nicholas) as his special friend but was cautious about the possibility of Nicholas going home with him for tea. Hamish was puzzled about the causes of Nicholas's difficulties but attributed these to 'the way he was born'. Hamish could not make any guesses about the future lives of Nicholas and his special school classmates. The special school was thought to be like the mainstream school but with 'easier lessons'.

Hamish worked with various children from the special school across the year of link sessions. He worked with both boys and girls but usually with boys. He was consistently clear and positive in the ways in which he worked with these children. He was very directive in his talk to special school work partners, gave few prompts or hints but tended to give explicit instructions. He also tended to describe what was happening, providing a running commentary as the two children worked together on the task. He asked few questions (fewer than any other of the Link 7 mainstream school children). He re-phrased comments more frequently than did other mainstream school children. Nearly one-third of everything that Hamish said to special school work partners was a re-phrasing or a repetition of an earlier comment within that sequence of talk. The high proportion of re-phrasings illustrates his persistence in trying to communicate with special school work partners. He had a strong tendency to re-phrase, not just repeat, a comment if it seemed not to have been understood. Hamish routinely divided tasks into small steps and gave frequent feedback, invariably positive and sometimes highly specific so that his work partner had a clear message about precisely what was good about his or her response. These characteristics made Hamish an effective tutor of special school children but his style was also highly controlling. Work partners had little room for initiative or taking direction.

After a year of link sessions I talked again with Hamish about his views of classmates and children from the special school. Children from the special school (Hamish used the phrase 'handicapped children') were still described in terms of presumed physical disabilities. Again, Hamish thought that the children from the special school were about 6 to 7 years old. He noted approvingly that they liked working. He described them as 'clever at some things – like painting'. This suggested that he accepted a double standard for these children, their painting was good for them, that is allowing for what he saw as their physical disabilities. Hamish was unusual among the Link 7 mainstream school children in articulating and accepting this double standard. After a year of experiences with children from the special school Hamish described them as needing only a little help with some things and not, as stated at the beginning of the year, a lot of help generally. Hamish was still slightly uncertain about having one of these children visit his home. The children from the special school were thought unlikely to recover from physical disabilities but were thought likely to get jobs (like a milkman) and to lead conventional adult lives. The special school (which had been visited once during the year) was described in very similar terms as at the start of the year, emphasising its similarity to the mainstream school but with easier lessons. Hamish said that he had enjoyed working with Nicholas and the other children because 'it helps them learn'.

DOMINANCE BY CHILDREN FROM THE MAINSTREAM SCHOOL

It is evident from the discussion of mainstream school children's guiding of special school work partners that the mainstream school children dominated the interaction. There were no instances in which the tables were turned and the special school children guided mainstream school children.

Features found to characterise the talk of mainstream school children in the Link 7 project included a number of aspects that have, in other research, been shown to distinguish the dominant conversational partner. These features included:

- making assumptions about the listener's needs ('Be careful, *he needs* to go slowly')
- directing comments to a third party ('Does *she* take sugar?')
- making assumptions about the listener's wishes ('*She wants* that')

- making assumptions about the listener's capabilities ('This is *too hard for you*')

Use of these strategies can be regarded as showing both that the mainstream school children saw themselves as dominant and that through these strategies they were covertly reinforcing their position. There were occasional examples of all these features in the mainstream school children's' talk to special school work partners, particularly that of Alice. Some of these features may be regarded as relatively positive. For example, to try to protect what are thought to be the other person's needs may be seen as supportive, as in the following example:

Adult (to Kirsty, from special school):	Go and wash again
Rachel (from mainstream school):	She just went and had a wash
Adult:	Go and have another one
Rachel (to Kirsty):	Come on then [sounding resigned]

This incident was supportive but Rachel made assumptions about Kirsty's wishes. Rachel did not ask Kirsty if she wanted to have another wash but assumed that she would not wish to do so. Rachel missed two chances here to ask Kirsty what she wanted to do.

Alice

One of the girls from the mainstream school (Alice) contrasted sharply with the other mainstream school children in her comparatively harsh dealings with special school work partners. She is discussed more fully here because of the implications for inclusive schools. She illustrated potential difficulties arising in the link projects. The nature of her interactions raises questions about integration and children, from mainstream or special schools, who have emotional problems or other serious difficulties in relating positively to a range of children. Alice was the youngest of two children in her family and had a sister four years older than herself. Alice was described by her teacher as being of average attainments compared with classmates. Prior to the link project the teacher had not been aware of any particular difficulties for Alice in getting on with other children. However, she was not generally popular with classmates.

At the start of the year I asked Alice about classmates whom she thought experienced difficulties at school. She named, without hesitation, six or seven children whom she described as poor at school tasks. She said that she disliked these children because they were naughty or 'bossy', they did not practise work at home and they forgot to return books to school. She thought that two things might change those children. One thing was more attention from their mothers and the other was for classmates to be more helpful. Alice thought that the future for those children was fairly bleak and that 'They'll probably only get jobs with a brush, sweepers'.

I also talked with Alice after she had worked for two sessions with children from the special school. She was emphatic that those children were different from herself and her classmates, including those with difficulties, because the children from the special school had 'something wrong with their brain'. She thought those children would not 'get better' and would not be able to live usual adult lives; for example, they would need to live in somebody else's house 'to be looked after'. Alice was the only mainstream school child, in either project, with this view of special school work partners. She described special school work partners as brave, for not crying when they got hurt, and as needing a lot of help.

During the link sessions Alice worked with various children from the special school, boys and girls, and had no strong preference for working with particular children. Equally, no special school child regularly chose Alice for a work partner. Direct instructions made up about one-third of all Alice's talk to special school work partners. This was about half the comparable figure for Hamish, discussed earlier. Alice always began, and sometimes continued with, a very direct style of instruction to work partners. This is illustrated in the following extract in which Alice worked with Melanie (age 6, from the special school). The two children were making print pictures using potatoes.

Alice:	Do it there ((pointing))
Melanie:	(no response)
Alice:	Do it
Melanie:	(no response)
Alice:	Do it there
Melanie:	(no response)
Alice:	Do it there
Melanie:	((prints the potato on the page as indicated by Alice))

Alice was not giving Melanie much help apart from repeating the instruction and pointing. She could, for example, have given an explanation (such as 'We've got a gap there') or described where to place the potato ('Put it at the top'). Alice had little feedback, apart from no response, from Melanie so she was forced to guess why Melanie was not responding. In the absence of any clear indication of what it was about the instruction that Melanie had not understood (or perhaps not heard) Alice repeated the short but adequate instruction. Alice seems to have been very inflexible in the way in which she worked with Melanie (and it was a typical feature of Alice's interactions with all the special school children).

When Alice was not being highly directive, as with Melanie, she tended to be too oblique. Her language style was often unhelpful to work partners because, in contrast to her apparently negative stereotype of those children's difficulties, she was often rather indirect in trying to guide those children through the task. This then led her to make irritable comments like 'You should have been able to do that'. Her style was erratic, veering from highly and overly directive to too oblique. Consequently work partners often appeared confused. At the times when they most needed direct help it was least forthcoming. Her re-phrasings were less frequent than Hamish's and, unlike Hamish, her re-phrasings sometimes made the comment more difficult for the work partner to understand, for example by making it much longer. Alice was on occasions very harsh in her dealings with children from the special school. She seemed to find any non-compliance, even mild, difficult to handle. She, unlike other children from the mainstream school, reprimanded special school children frequently and forcibly. She also recounted incidents of supposed misbehaviour to other children:

> (to Michelle, mainstream school classmate) 'She's [Lucy] been a naughty girl. Guess what she did over there? When she had finished with the dolly and stuff she sat on the floor and she would not budge a muscle.'

After a year of link sessions I talked again with Alice about her views concerning classmates thought to have difficulties and children from the special school. Classmates with difficulties were again readily named. Their supposed difficulties were still attributed to naughtiness and lack of concentration. Alice thought that these children tried hard occasionally but would have to try even harder if they were to catch up with other children in the class.

She described special school children in relation
haviour and emphasised that these children had
normal' and 'acted more silly' over the year of the
Perhaps by this she meant that they had not mad
progress she expected of her mainstream school clas .... .mce
estimated that special school work partners were about 6 years old
(a broadly accurate guess) and different from mainstream school
children because, as stated at the start of the year, they had something wrong with their brains. These children were thought to work
hard even though they were 'not very clever'. Working hard was
an important explanation of cleverness/attainment for Alice but
unusually for her age, Alice accepted that hard work and high
attainments did not necessarily go together. Whereas some classmates had low attainments through not working hard, other
children (from the special school) worked hard but still had low
attainments. Conceptually, this was an advanced idea as many
young children tend to assume that positive characteristics go
together (clever children work hard, attractive people are clever,
etc.) and do not recognise as possible the type of mismatch described by Alice.

Alice's interactions with children from the special school needed
to be very closely monitored and she needed some specific help
with working constructively with other children. Her dominance,
close to bullying occasionally, of special school children was not
parallelled, according to the class teacher, in Alice's interactions
with mainstream school classmates. The latent bullying emerged
with weaker or younger children but was curbed with peers. The
more one looks at how Alice interacted with other children the
more it seems that she was herself a child with difficulties. She had
problems relating positively to other children and the link project
highlighted these difficulties. The classroom which focuses on
meeting individual children's needs will need to respond positively to many and varied individual differences.

TENSION IN SPECIAL SCHOOL PUPILS' INTERACTIONS
WITH MAINSTREAM SCHOOL CHILDREN

We have seen that the mainstream school children tended to dominate verbal interaction. However, special school pupils were not
always accepting of mainstream school pupils' dominance. Special
school pupils exercised various strategies, mainly non-verbal, to

assert themselves. In the following extract Lucy (age 6, from special school) resisted Alice's attempts to dominate. Lucy did not have the linguistic skills to explain that she did not want to cooperate with Alice but she made that view evident through her non-verbal behaviour.

Alice:	Lucy STAND UP
	[said very firmly, crossly but quietly]
Lucy:	((sitting down, arms crossed))
Alice:	I'll leave you
	And you're not going to play me up the way you were, are you?
	Not going to be moody
	Right
Lucy:	((not moving))
	((sticking tongue out at Alice))
Alice:	Stick that tongue back in or
	[lowering voice]
	I'll chop it out for dinner
	WOULD YOU DO THE DRAWING
	I came over here for *you* to have some fun
	You *don't* think you're going to get away with it
	Cos you're not
	You're gonna draw your picture
Adult:	[Adult intervening]
	That one's done
Alice:	[to Lucy] [muttering]
	You should have been able to do that by heart

Here Alice's apparent frustration with Lucy may have reflected Alice's overexpectations. She apparently expected Lucy to have been able to complete the picture with ease ('by heart').

In the Link 7 project, three of the special school children (Joanna, Melanie and David) accounted for most of the attempts at self-assertiveness by special school children. These happened relatively frequently with Alice who behaved in an, at least superficially, dominant way. It was as if she pushed special school work partners to the point at which they finally refused to comply and, uncharacteristically, rebelled. In so doing the special school children had to summon up both linguistic and social resources.

Tension also arose on a few occasions on which special school children, resisting mainstream school children's dominance, asserted their positions verbally. When these special school children defended their positions in this way they were pushed, in the views of their special school teachers, to use more complex language and clearer articulation than was usual for them. This was illustrated when Michelle (age 6, from the mainstream school) and Joanna (age 6, from the special school) played at dressing up:

Michelle:	D'you want a dress on?
	Want this on?
	D'you want to be a nurse?
Joanna:	Yes
Michelle:	Right let me do it then
Joanna:	(?) [not interpretable]
Michelle:	What?
Joanna:	Want to be a doctor
Michelle:	No
Joanna:	Yes
Michelle:	Might
Joanna:	Might

Dialogue had been recorded before the start of this dressing up game and there had been no mention of doctors until Joanna introduced it here. This shows that she was able to draw on knowledge from outside the situation (the relative status of doctors and nurses) and apply it in the course of this game. Four minutes after the end of this extract, Michelle again raised the suggestion that Joanna dress up as a nurse. Joanna still maintained that she did not want to be a nurse. She eventually did agree to play the nurse but only after Michelle had tempted her with a very colourful, glittery piece of fabric and said 'Oooh look, that's for nurse'. When Joanna's special school teachers heard the tape recording of this extract they expressed surprise at the length and clarity of Joanna's statement 'Want to be a doctor'. This was apparently an unusually long and complex utterance compared with her usual talk in school. The incident illustrates the negotiation of roles involved if one child or the other does not accept the role imposed by their partner. Here 'role' can be taken literally but the same point applies in the more general sense of partner / guide roles.

CONCLUSION

In summary, young mainstream school children dominated the

interaction with special school work partners. Special school pupils were given many instructions (of varying directness) with few questions and few explanations about how or why to carry out the task. Mainstream school children seemed to find it difficult, or not to recognise the need, to stand back from the task and let the special school child take over, even if this meant that child making mistakes. Interestingly, this standing back was rare even though teachers often reminded the children from the mainstream school that they were not to do too much for the special school children. The large majority of the mainstream school children were enabling and not domineering in their dominance of the interaction.

For the special school children, the link sessions appear to have provided opportunities, not just for learning specific tasks, but for developing linguistic and social skills which were not drawn out in day to day interactions with other special school pupils. They had, in the mainstream school children, models of language and behaviour not found among children in the special school. It is interesting to speculate on what the mainstream school children may have been learning about the nature of communication specifically, in the link project. The lack of understanding of many special school children may have pushed the mainstream school children into thinking about a range of ways of communicating (verbally and non-verbally) and, in particular, to work at successive rephrasings of a comment. For both groups the link project provided a diversity of, probably unique for them, linguistic and social experiences. These experiences broke through some of the expression/interpretation barriers suggested by Paul Williams as preventing effective communication between non-disabled people and people with learning difficulties.

There are two groups of changes which make 11 year olds more effective, in general, than 7 year olds when it comes to tutoring other pupils. One set of changes concerns the development of specific strategies, such as giving explanations. The older child tutors increasingly support instructions and corrections with explanations. This is very helpful to the partner as adding an explanation is related directly to better learning. Another important change is the increased ability to plan ahead and to think strategically about how a task may be accomplished. This strategic thinking makes the tutor more flexible and so potentially more responsive to a partner. The child tutor is not holding only one series of moves in mind. Older children are also more effective than younger children at recovering the partner's attention after distractions, especially if these have lasted some while. Although older children make competent child tutors, especially in relation to problem solving, they lack some adult tutoring skills. One contrast between children and adults in tutoring is that adults often provide reflective assessments at the end of the task. Children rarely seem to provide this review of how accomplishment on the task has compared with initial goals.

These specific changes in tutoring skills during middle childhood relate to a broader point. This concerns the child's ability to cope with the collection of demands embodied in any tutoring task. These demands include social (for example, being polite), linguistic (for example, using vocabulary that the partner is likely to understand), managerial (for example, collecting the resources needed for the task), manipulative (for example, handling scissors skilfully) and cognitive (understanding the task) aspects. A variety of research has investigated how children distribute their limited cognitive resources when tutoring. A new task taught to an unknown child in an unfamiliar situation will be much more taxing for the tutor than if one or more of those elements is familiar. Broadly, as children go through middle childhood they become increasingly competent in dealing concurrently with these various demands. These points are relevant to analyses of interactions between pupils in the Link 11 project, discussed in the following chapter.

Chapter 5

Working together
The Link 11 Project

> Jane, who is 14 and attends a school for pupils with severe learning difficulties (SLD), is working with Jenny, an 11 year old, who attends a mainstream school. They are writing a story together using a micro-computer. After an hour they have produced a joint story alongside pictures of themselves and some labels for the work which is to go in the school entrance hall. Jane has talked very little but Jenny has often stood back from the task, letting Jane take the lead.

This chapter looks in detail at the types of interaction in this kind of situation among children and young people in the later years of primary, or early years of secondary, schooling. In particular, this chapter looks at how interactions at this age range differ from those of the younger children described in Chapter 4. The material is organised around a discussion of four target special school pupils. These pupils were identified at random from the group of nine 12 to 15 year olds from the special school involved in the Link 11 project.

OVERVIEW OF COMMUNICATION IN THE LINK 11 PROJECT

Video recording in the Link 11 project concentrated on four of the special school pupils and the mainstream school children with whom they worked during weekly link sessions over one school year. During the first half of the year (eighteen weekly sessions) the pupils worked in pairs or, occasionally, threesomes. Each of the sessions included around nine special and twelve mainstream school pupils. A total of 32 mainstream school pupils were involved during the year. Pupils had a free choice of partner(s) and, allowing for occasional pupil absences, kept the same work partners for at least six weeks. There was a very strong bias towards working with pupils of one's own sex. The small working groups were made up of one or two mainstream, and one special, school pupils. Although there were some differences between talk in pairs or threesomes the findings from both types of group have been combined here because the differences were not so substantial as to change the points being made. Recordings of interactions, as in the Link 7 project, focused on periods during which the pupils were working closely together. These interactions may not have been typical of how the pupils related to one another in other contexts. (During the last half of the year pupils worked in larger groups (six to eight pupils in total, including some young people from the school's unit for pupils with profound and multiple learning difficulties). Only brief reference is made to interactions during this period. Unless specified otherwise, findings in this chapter refer to the interactions in pairs or threesomes, i.e. during the first half of the year.)

Interactions and their contexts were coded (from video, supplemented with audio, and observational recordings) every five seconds for each of the four target pupils in each session to provide an overview of the interaction. The coded time ranged from a total of fifteen to twenty-five minutes in any one of the eighteen link sessions for each target special school pupil. For each five second point a note was made of which pupil (if any) was speaking, to whom the pupil was speaking and at what or whom each pupil was looking. These aspects of talk and gaze were grouped in relation to the roles of special and mainstream pupils. For example, categories included: a special school pupil speaking or gesturing to a mainstream school work partner, special and mainstream school pupils communicating simultaneously to one another and/or looking at one another, and a child from the mainstream school looking at an adult. There were few occasions on which mainstream school children were speaking to, or looking at, one another and those data have been omitted here. In addition, because of unreliability in coding data about whether pupils were attending to a joint focus when not communicating with one another, that information is also not reported here. It is difficult to be sure from video material made in a classroom using a mobile camera at what exactly a pupil is looking. There was no such variability about the other aspects coded here.

Overall, interaction with adults was low during the pairs or small group working because adults deliberately stayed in the background. In contrast, special school pupils' interactions with adults were disproportionately high during the larger group sessions in the second half of the year (not reported in detail here). This may have reflected the more frequent presence of adults in the larger group but may also reflect how strongly attracted the special school pupils were to adults. This may have been indicative of home backgrounds in which, for many of these pupils, adults, not young children, predominated. This has implications for how link sessions are staffed and suggests that there are disadvantages in having a large number of adults present.

Systematic sub-samples from the interactions between each of the four target special school pupils and their work partners from the mainstream school were also collected and coded. The purpose of these sub-samples was to look in more detail at the nature of the communication, non-verbal as well as verbal, between special and mainstream school pupils. We wanted to find out more about what the special school pupils were doing than we had been able to do in the Link 7 project. There, because of the use of audio data alone, the roles of the special school pupils were underemphasised. Communication sub-samples in the Link 11 project were of fifteen minutes duration for each target special school pupil in each of twelve sessions. The fifteen minute period was made up of three five-minute slices of time. These were coded for the nature of the communication (verbal or non-verbal), numbers and types of turns in the conversation for each pupil, length of turns, length of comments, repetitions and re-phrasings within speech topics, and function of comments. The last two categories used structures employed in the Link 7 project analysis.

The young people from the special school involved in the Link 11 project were more vocal than were the younger special school children involved in the Link 7 project. Although the older pupils said more, much of what they said could not be interpreted clearly. About one-fifth of the Link 11 special school pupils' talk was not coded for content or structure because it was not possible to interpret exactly what was said. Overall, mainstream school children in the Link 11 project said three times as much as did their special school work partners. So although, as in the Link 7 project, mainstream school children dominated the talk, this was less marked with the older pupils. In eighteen weeks of video-recorded small group interaction there were (in the sub-samples described earlier) nearly a thousand comments by mainstream school to special school pupils and 325 comments by special to mainstream school pupils. As I go on to discuss in this chapter, there were large differences between individual special school pupils. The predominant style of interaction, as in the Link 7 project, was of mainstream school children guiding, and more explicitly tutoring, special school pupils.

SPECIAL SCHOOL PUPILS' INTERACTIONS WITH MAINSTREAM SCHOOL WORK PARTNERS

In general, children with learning difficulties develop in broadly similar ways to non-disabled children although development is slower and with greater variability in the speed of development (McTear and Conti-Ramsden, 1992). (See further reading on language development.) Generalisations about language development in children with learning difficulties are probably not valid for the reasons outlined in Chapter 1 concerning the heterogeneity of learning difficulties. For that reason, the four target special school pupils are discussed individually.

Jane

Jane was 14 years old at the start of the year of link sessions. She was of normal size for her chronological age and had one older sister. Jane had unknown causes of severe learning difficulties and was on medication to control epileptic seizures. She attended local Girl Guides and could do a little reading and writing. She was very friendly in her manner towards other people (children and adults), hugging and stroking them. Her teachers reported that Jane particularly liked being with adults. Jane always worked with girls during the first eighteen weeks of the Link 11 project. She said that she liked working with children from the mainstream school and, as a result of this link project, she became a regular attender (for part of each school week) at the mainstream school.

By including non-verbal as well as verbal communication in the analysis of interaction, a more balanced picture of interaction emerges in the Link 11 than in the Link 7 project. The proportion of time during which Jane was speaking or gesturing was similar to that in which mainstream school work partners were speaking. About one-sixth of the time sampled was spent in Jane communicating with a mainstream school work partner. The same proportion of the time was spent in a child from the mainstream school communicating with Jane. Jane, unlike her mainstream school work partners, spent time interacting with adults (although not a great deal of time – 4 per cent of the time sampled). There were few points at which Jane and her mainstream school work partners were looking at one another directly. The unreported time was spent either independently or working together but not looking at one another.

Focusing on communication between Jane and her mainstream school work partners, it is clear that there was enormous variability between sessions. This reflects different activities and, to some extent, different work partners. TÀ
#:he variability shows that it is useful to monitor a range of situations when 'integration' is evaluated. There were no joint outside breaks during these link sessions so this period, which would also have been interesting to monitor, did not arise. Overall, Jane took nearly half of all the conversational turns when working on shared tasks with mainstream school children. This figure includes non-verbal turns, such as nodding her head. It was not the case that Jane was simply the passive recipient of the mainstream school children's talk. Jane was making a substantial contribution to the interaction.

About one-fifth of Jane's turns in the conversation were non-verbal only. Interestingly, nearly one-third of the turns of Jane's mainstream school work partners were also non-verbal (with or without speech as well). Often their non-verbal communication was supplemented with speech, so reinforcing the message. It seems that they instinctively used non-verbal communication, perhaps because Jane responded to this. We would need to monitor children in more detail and in similar situations with a variety of work partners in order to check this out. If it is so then it suggests that mainstream school children may have been prompted in interesting ways to make use of non-verbal communication. Perhaps the link sessions were fostering a 'bilingualism' (i.e. use of a range of verbal and non-verbal communication) in mainstream school pupils in contrast to a greater use of oral communication in the mainstream school.

Verbal turns in the conversation, for Jane and for her mainstream school work partners, were rarely more than one comment long. The range in terms of the length of individual comments was similar for Jane and her work partners. Comments for all these pupils ranged between one and seven morphemes in length (for example, 'Shall we go on painting?' – six morphemes (a morpheme is a unit of meaning)). So although Jane said slightly less overall, there was not a large gap in the amount said by her and that said by her work partners. However, the mean length of comments was slightly higher (3.7 morphemes) for the mainstream school children than for Jane (the mean length of her comments was 2.1 morphemes).

How did mainstream school work partners respond to a comment from Jane? Jane's comments can be divided between those that started a new conversation topic and those that continued a topic which was already 'on the go'. Figure 16 shows the responses of children from the mainstream school to a comment from one of the target special school pupils. This figure classifies the comments and responses in one of four ways according to whether the special school pupil's comment started a new speech topic or whether it continued a topic from the work partner. Then each of these are divided according to whether the work partner from the mainstream school then made a response (verbal or non-verbal) or gave no response.

Approximately three-quarters of Jane's comments were continuing a topic, following on from what a mainstream school child had said. For example:

Debbie: Shall we go on painting?
Jane: Done all

This suggests that Jane was working at keeping the conversation going. Most (86 per cent) of these types of comment were followed up by Jane's work partner(s) from the mainstream school. This shows that they too were generally keeping the conversation going even though at times it was difficult to interpret Jane's comments. It was more difficult for them when she introduced a new conversation topic. However, nearly half of her initiations of conversation topics also received a response from the mainstream school child. This indicates a positive picture of an exchange of talk with, for the most part, each pupil trying to respond to the other. (See Lewis and Carpenter, 1990, for a similar point concerning interactions between younger special and mainstream school children.)

The next aspect of talk to consider is the function of what was being said. This can be assessed using the same structure as that

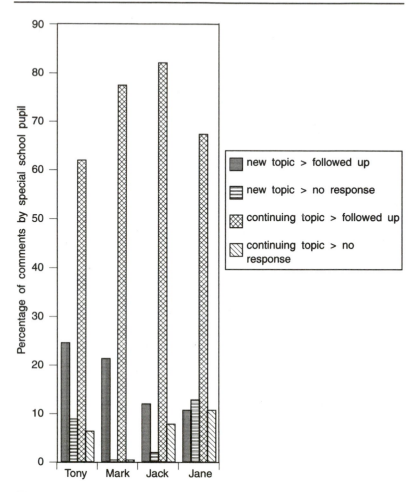

Figure 16 Link 11 project: the responses of mainstream school pupils to comments by a special school pupil

used to analyse talk by the mainstream school children involved in the Link 7 project. However, in the Link 11 project we have data about talk from both sides in the interaction as these special school pupils were more vocal and articulate than were the 4- to 8-year-old special school children in the Link 7 project. This is reflected in Figure 17 which shows the pattern of talk given and received by

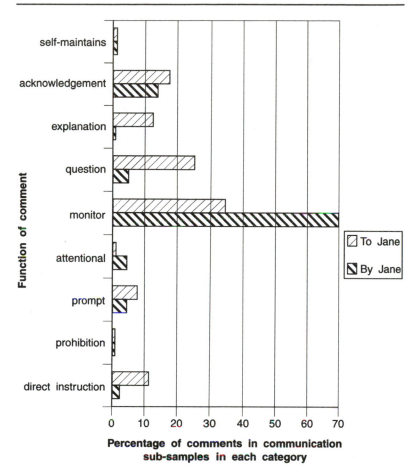

Figure 17 Talk by and to Jane
For key, see notes to Figure 13, page 81

Jane when working with mainstream school pupils on a shared task.

This shows that Jane's talk to her work partners was slightly less varied, in terms of these functional categories, than was their talk to her. About two-thirds of all Jane's talk was in the form of a running commentary on what was happening. In comparison, about one-third of the talk by her work partners from the mainstream school children was of this type. Jane often affirmed or acknowledged a comment or action from her work partner (often this acknowledgement was brief, like 'uh uh', to signal agreement). This kind of response was similarly frequent in talk to Jane from her work partners indicating an attentiveness to one another.

The mainstream school children differed from Jane in three main ways here. First, they asked far more questions of her than she did of them. Most of their questions were closed questions with a very limited range of potential answers (often just yes or no). Arguably, it would have been helpful for an adult explicitly to encourage these mainstream school children to ask more open questions and for Jane to have been helped to formulate questions which she could have asked. Second, the mainstream school children offered explanations far more often than did Jane. Their giving of explanations is likely to have been a very helpful strategy as it made an instruction more generalisable. For example, it is more helpful to be told 'We could put yellow [paint] in the red [paint] because that will make orange' than to be told just 'We could put yellow [paint] in the red [paint]'. As noted in the previous chapter, the Link 7 mainstream school children rarely gave explanations like this.

On one occasion Jane gave an explanation to her work partner from the mainstream school:

| Mandy (mainstream school pupil): | I'll take this one back ((picking up completed sheet of shapes)) |
| Jane: | Yeh cos we've done some there now |

An interesting feature of Jane's explanation is that it was tagged to Mandy's comment. The explanation concerned why Mandy was moving the sheet of paper, not Jane's own actions. As such it illustrates a point at which the two pupils were closely coordinating both their speech and their activities.

A third difference between Jane's talk and that of her work partners was in the giving of instructions. Jane received a number of instructions but, as can be seen by comparing the proportion of direct instructions and prompts received, many of these instructions were given as hints. This contrasts with the younger mainstream school children in the Link 7 project who were much more overtly directive with special school work partners. Direct forms of instruction were used by Jane's work partners when, as in the following example, a task had proved difficult. It was then taught by breaking it down into its components, systematically teaching each element. In the following example, Debbie was trying to help Jane to make a puppet.

Debbie:	Cut round here
	(no response)
	You cut out round that bit
	[re-phrased, emphasising Jane's role]
	(no response)
	You cut this bit, right?
	[re-phrased, and question]
Jane:	((nodding))
Debbie:	Cut along the lines
	[instruction, reference to where to cut]
	Start there
	[instruction, reference to where to commence]
Jane:	((cutting out))

Debbie twice re-phrased her first instruction, to cut out some fabric. When Jane still did not respond, Debbie sub-divided the task. She pointed out where to cut, referring to markers ('along the lines'), and then emphasised where to begin ('start there').

There were no examples of Jane repeating a comment to a work partner and very few examples of her re-phrasing a comment. She was representative of the special school pupils in this respect. In the following, unusual, exchange, Jane gave a prompt to Danielle. When Danielle made no response Jane softened the prompt. This emphasised the tentativeness of the suggestion and avoided appearing too assertive:

Jane:	You could stick them there
	((gluing paper pieces on a large picture))
Danielle:	(no response)
Jane:	If you want to
Danielle:	Yes

Jane's first instruction ('You could stick them there') was tentative and indirect. It contrasted with the types of instruction she tended to receive from mainstream school children (for example, 'Stick them there').

Jane received few repetitions or re-phrasings from her work partners. These mainstream school pupils tended to change the task, not the instruction, if special school pupils seemed not to understand the activity. Jane's work partners would occasionally check that she had sub-skills for a task:

Bobbie: That's in blue
             Which one's blue?

This illustrates a typical switching between task instructions and checking for sub-skills. A similar sensitivity in helping Jane through a task was shown by Tracey when they were making 'rubbings' pictures using surfaces around the school:

Tracey: [holding Jane's hand against the wooden surface]
             Rough or smooth?
             Is it rough or smooth?
             [re-phrasing]
Jane: HI YER!
             ((calling to friend))
             [distracted]
Tracey: You *feel* that
             [involving Jane]
             What does it feel like?
Jane: Smooth
Tracey: Or rough?
             [prompting]
Jane: Don't know
             Rough
             [picking up cue]
Tracey: yeh
             It's not very . . .?
             [raised question tone]
             [checking understanding?]
Jane: Heater's on too
             [distracted]
Tracey: Yeh
             [abandoning teaching sequence]
             Do another one?

Tracey knew the answer and tried to prompt Jane towards the correct response in several ways:

1   By getting her to feel the surface.
2   By presenting alternatives ('Is it rough or smooth?').
3   When Jane gave the wrong answer Tracey ignored this but

cued her in with a simple closed question requiring only yes or no for an answer: 'Or [is it] rough?' Jane seems to have taken this as a hint that 'rough' was the required answer but Tracey continued her teaching sequence by

4   Apparently checking whether Jane had really understood the term 'rough' or was just imitating Tracey. So Tracey asked 'It's not very . . .?' but Jane seems to have become tired with this work sequence and interested in other things. Tracey responded to this by abandoning that teaching sequence and suggesting 'Do another one?'

The sequence illustrates an adjustment to what kinds of teaching prompts Jane seemed to need and an ability to gauge when not to persist with a particular task.

Interestingly, there was one instance in which Jane supported one of her work partners (Bobbie) against another mainstream school child (Danielle) while they were making a collage together:

Bobbie:	[to Danielle]
	Stick a few more round here
Jane:	((watching Bobbie and Danielle))
Danielle:	((gluing pieces))
	Finished then!
Bobbie:	There's another one
	[pointing out task not finished]
Danielle:	That's enough Bobbie
	We've got enough
	[resisting Bobbie's implied instruction]
Bobbie:	No
Danielle:	No Bobbie
	That's enough
	Can't fit all these on
	[giving explanation]
Bobbie:	Yeh, put that there, the little ones
	[justifying implied instruction]
Jane:	[to Danielle]
	You can stick that little one here
	[supporting Bobbie's suggestion]
Danielle:	((sticking piece on but not where Jane had suggested))

Jane showed considerable social and linguistic skills in taking the initiative in supporting Bobbie's suggestion but in an understated fashion. Danielle half-responded to Jane's suggestion, sticking the piece on, but not where Jane had indicated.

Tony

Tony was 15 years old at the start of the year of link sessions and was slightly small for his chronological age. He had a brother and a sister, both of whom were much younger than him. There was no known cause for Tony's severe learning difficulties and he was not on medication. Outside school, he enjoyed spending time with adults in his extended family and close family friends. He enjoyed listening to music and going on family trips to the country. Tony's spoken language was clear, well structured and used a wide vocabulary. However, the superficial impression of high language skills was misleading as Tony was skilful in repeating what he had heard but understood comparatively little of what was said to him. Consequently on initial contact he gave the deceptive impression of understanding much more than was the case. Tony was talkative and gregarious. He was friendly towards classroom visitors and appeared to enjoy being with people. After the Link 11 project he began a series of work experience placements in which he worked in local firms for part of each school week.

Tony spent a substantial proportion of the shared activity time during link sessions talking to mainstream school work partners, or being addressed by them. He comes across therefore as being sociable and outgoing in these sessions. In about one-quarter of the observation points Tony was talking to one of his work partners and in approximately half the observation points he was being spoken to. There was no interaction between adults and Tony's mainstream school work partners and very little (under 5 per cent) between Tony and adults. So Tony and his work partners were giving one another a lot of attention.

Tony always worked with two boys from the mainstream school. Although the identities of these children varied, his pattern of interaction was remarkably similar across the sessions. In every session, he occupied over 40 per cent of the conversational turns. ('Turns' includes both verbal and non-verbal turns, such as making a gesture or sign.) As Tony was always one of three participants it could be argued that he was actually holding more than his 'fair' share of the conversation. Tony had more non-verbal turns than did the mainstream school children. Just under 10 per cent of his turns, but under 1 per cent of theirs, were non-verbal (with or without speech as well). These children may have been influenced by Tony's apparently high verbal skills in not using non-verbal communication alone even though this may have been what Tony needed. There were a number of instances in which Tony misinterpreted an apparently simple instruction from his work partner who may have been misled into believing that, because of what Tony had said, he would understand the comment. An illustration of this occurred during a session in which Michael was measuring Tony's body prior to them making a large self-portait of each pupil:

Tony: I like measuring I do
              [introducing the word 'measuring']
Michael: I'll measure up your arm
Tony: ((raising the arm furthest away from Michael into the
              air))

Tony seemed to respond to the words 'up' arm' but his actions were inappropriate in the context of what Michael was intending to do. Before this, Michael had been measuring things on the table top so, had Tony understood the comment, the logical reaction would have been to place his nearest arm to Michael on the table top. There were also some slightly bizarre responses from Tony:

Martin: I want to get a computer this Christmas
              What do you want for this Christmas Tony?
Tony: My dreams come true at Christmas

and later:

Martin: There, that's Father Christmas done
              ((having made a fabric model))
Tony: It's the alternative Mrs Christmas

These comments by Tony may have been echoes of phrases he had heard from adults but he had some notion of when they were appropriate and thus seemed to confuse his mainstream school work partners about how much he was understanding.

Verbal turns by Tony and his mainstream school work partners were rarely more than one comment long. The length of these comments was from one to eleven morphemes for Tony and from one to fourteen morphemes for his mainstream school work partners. This is longer than was found among talk by Jane and her work partners and reinforces the impression that Tony and his partners were comparatively talkative. There was only a small difference between the mean length of comments by Tony and those by his mainstream school work partners (the mean length of comments was 3.3 and 3.9 morphemes for Tony and his work partners (grouped) respectively). This points to a relative similarity in terms of the amount said by the pupils in any one conversational turn.

One-third of Tony's comments started a new conversational topic while the other two-thirds took over a topic started by a child from the mainstream school (see Figure 16). The relatively high proportion of new topics meant that Tony's work partners had to be lively conversationally in order to keep up with his recurrent changes of focus. Tony introduced more new conversational topics than did any of the other target special school pupils. As with Jane, about three-quarters of new topics were followed up by work partners. This says much for their attention and tolerance given the frequency, repetition and quantity of these new topics. About one in eight of Tony's comments received no response from work partners.

The introduction of new topics posed a dilemma for the mainstream school children. Should they respond to this topic and risk taking Tony's attention off the task or should they ignore the new topic? When Tony introduced a new and unrelated conversation topic his work partners tended to follow the topic for a short while and then to draw Tony back to the task. This happened in the following extract in which Tony, during work with Michael and Greg, started to talk about holidays while they were making 'rubbings' pictures using surfaces around the school:

Greg:	Try that
	((handing Tony crayon))
Tony:	You been to Poppy?
	[a holiday centre]
	[introduces new topic]
Greg:	No
	[answers Tony's question,
	no continuation of the topic]
Tony:	They got three parks at Poppy
	[continuing Poppy topic]
Michael:	D'you want to go to Poppy?

	[continuing Poppy topic]
Tony:	I like Poppy
	[no direct response to Michael]
	It's nice, Poppy
	Holiday camps
	[amplifying what is at Poppy]
	Lots there
	Chalets
	Caravans
	I like Poppy
	[repetition]
	I got a Poppy book at home
Greg:	Have you?
	[responding to topic]
Tony:	Yeh
	[answering Greg's question]
	I'll bring it to show you tomorrow
	[following up Greg's question]
	Next week
	[self-correction]
	Have you got Poppy Holidays [book] at home?
Greg:	No
	[responding to Tony's question]
	We don't go there
	[and explaining]
Michael:	I'll go to the holiday shop
	[extending topic]
Tony:	Do you?
	[accepting, but not developing, Michael's (mis-heard?) initiation]
	Poppy's ever so big
	[reiterating point]
	Poppy Holidays
Greg:	Want to use green?
	[returning Tony's focus to the topic]
	((handing Tony green crayon))

This sequence lasted one and a half minutes and was one of a series of digressions in which Tony introduced a succession of topics about which he talked repeatedly. Tony, Greg and Michael had had virtually identical conversations to this several times. However,

Greg and Michael still responded to Tony's questions and comments about Poppy Holidays with apparent interest. They did not curtail the topic immediately but after a short while returned Tony's attention to the task. For his part, Tony responded to two of the three topic-related responses from Greg or Michael and developed one of these responses.

Special school pupils' comments which were unrelated to the task often concerned personal information or preferences. This was in sharp contrast to the mainstream school children. They almost never made this sort of remark, solicited or unsolicited. The only comment about personal feelings, from any of the mainstream school pupils recorded in the Link 11 projects, was from Michael. This was in direct response to a question from Tony:

Tony: Do you get cross sometimes at school?
            [introducing new topic]
Michael: Yes [softly]
            A lot
            [extending response]
            [. . . . . long pause]
            ((returning to task))

The function of the talk by and to Tony is summarised in Figure 18.

Tony's talk to his work partners was divided between giving a running commentary, asking questions and acknowledging comments from his work partners. Tony repeatedly questioned anyone with whom he worked. Nearly one-quarter of all his talk to mainstream school work partners was in the form of questions, some of which were open questions. Tony's questions, duplicated across many work partners as well as adults, included:

'Do you know Father Christmas?'

'Is Elvis good?'

'Is it holidays now?'

Tony was not satisfied with a brief answer to his questions but followed them up with requests for more details. For example, he asked many children if they had been to Poppy Holidays; any child who said 'yes' was then asked for details of when, where and their reactions to specific aspects of the holiday.

Tony's questions were part of his distractability. His concentration lapses were shown in other ways also and were ended

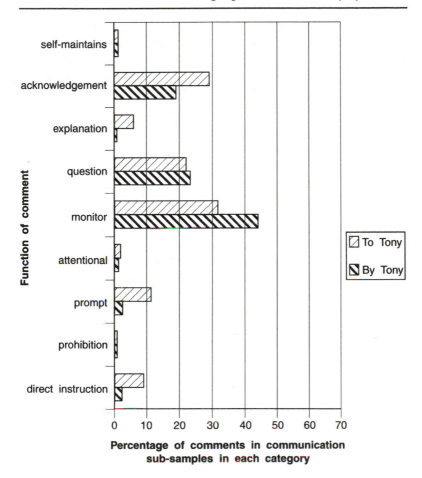

Figure 18 Talk by and to Tony
For key, see note to Figure 13, page 81

unobtrusively by his work partners in several ways. Attention was regained by nudging him, saying his name and / or drawing attention to the task by touching or moving the materials. This was usually all that was needed to bring Tony's attention back to the activity. The mainstream school children appeared proficient and sensitive to the need to do this and Tony's attention rarely wandered from the task for long.

The overall pattern of talk was broadly similar for Tony and for his mainstream school work partners. However, mainstream school children, unlike Tony, also gave instructions (directly and also indirectly as prompts) and explanations. Tony rarely gave these. Slightly more of the instructions to Tony from his work partners were given as prompts than as direct instructions. Tony usually responded to prompts:

Michael: OK, let's put that on Tony
Tony: I will that
             ((moving piece))

Tony's work partners offered a series of prompts when Tony seemed to run into persistent difficulties:

Michael: What's *this* Tony?
             ((showing Tony a piece of a large jigsaw of a boy))
             What *part of his body's* that?
Greg: What *part of his body* d'you think that is?
             D'you think it's his *arm*?
             [NB arm = correct answer]

In Michael's and Greg's re-phrasing, the changes focused the teaching point, narrowing the potential answers in a way that made it increasingly likely that Tony would respond correctly.

Repetitions within a speech topic were rare in Tony's talk (2 per cent of all talk to his work partners) and non-existent in that of his work partners. Re-phrasings were also infrequent (also 2 per cent of all talk to his work partners). The effect of his re-phrasings was to drop the least crucial parts of the comment, for example:

             Do you come from Greenfields School do you?
             [no response]
             Do you come from Greenfields School?

However, Tony often failed to recognise when a re-phrasing was needed:

Tony: D'you like Cliff Richard?
Daniel: Yes
Tony: Played with The Shadows didn't he?
Daniel: (. . . .)
             Shadows?
Tony: I like Cliff Richard

Tony's work partners occasionally re-phrased comments to him.

These tended to lengthen a comment, as if making amendments on the run, rather than pausing, and giving a re-phrasing:

'That's how big your body is (.) for all of you (.) *your legs as well*' (Michael to Tony when showing Tony a piece of string used to measure Tony's height prior to making a life size portrait of each pupil)

They may have done this, rather than doing as Link 7 mainstream school children had done and shortening a comment in the re-phrasing, because of Tony's superficially strong verbal skills. This lengthening of comments accounts in part for the relatively long comments to Tony by his work partners. They did not seem to assume that Tony would need brief instructions. Their clarifications increased what Tony had to remember but he was often able to cope with this, completing tasks successfully.

Occasionally talk to Tony showed that mainstream school partners were underestimating him. In the following extract Greg and Michael had just completed a jigsaw, ostensibly with Tony's help, but having completed most of the jigsaw without him. Tony then asserted his own position:

Tony:	I can do it on my own I can
	Just watch me
Greg:	OK you try and do it on your own
	[implied scepticism]
Michael:	What would you like to do now Tony?
	[ignoring Tony's wish to do the task alone]
Tony:	I'm going to do this
	((moving jigsaw pieces))
	[reiterating intention to do task]
Michael:	We'll help you a bit then Tony
	[not standing back from the task]
Tony:	I'll do it
	I know what to do with these
	[reiterating intention and ability to do task]

In this extract Tony had to reiterate his intention of completing the jigsaw task. Greg and Michael's comments suggest that they did not expect Tony to be able to complete the task on his own. In the event, Tony re-assembled the jigsaw quickly and correctly. Greg and Michael, rather patronisingly, then praised Tony for completing the task correctly. Tony, more than any of the other young people from the special school, often held his own with his work partners and, uniquely in the link projects data, mildly insulted a child from the mainstream school:

Michael: (Put your?) hand on there
              ((moving jigsaw piece himself))
              Oops
              [piece seen to be in the wrong place]
              Oh no, sorry
Tony: Oh God! You wally!
Michael: [muttering] Yes I'm a wally

Mark

Mark was 12 years old at the start of the year of link sessions and, like Tony, had a brother and a sister both of whom were much younger than himself. Mark's severe learning difficulties were caused by trauma at birth and he was not on medication. He seemed to have few interests outside school apart from watching television. Mark's spoken language was limited to vocalisations and occasional recognisable words. He often used non-verbal gestures and Makaton signs, rather than speech, to communicate. Mark was initially shy in his manner towards people he did not know well but, in contrast to Tony, developed very close relationships with a small number of people. This was evident in the link sessions in which he worked mainly with girls from the mainstream school and became closely attached to one or two whom he would chase, hug and kiss.

As would be expected from this profile of Mark, there was relatively little talk in his interactions with mainstream school work partners. Overall, the proportion of observed time points at which Mark was communicating verbally with a work partner was low (just over 8 per cent) but his work partners were talking to him for nearly one-quarter of the observations. So there was a large difference here with, on the surface, mainstream school children working at communicating with Mark while he was, verbally, much more reticent. Neither Mark nor his work partners communicated much with adults (under 2 per cent for any child). There were also very few occasions during which Mark and his work partners were looking at one another (2 per cent). To gain from the link sessions Mark probably needed to develop both social and communication skills.

There was an increase in communication between Mark and his work partners both across a single session and across a series of sessions as Mark got to know his work partners. There was an equal balance of input (verbal and/or non-verbal) from Mark and his work partners in the communication sub-samples. Overall, this was exactly evenly divided between Mark and his work partners (combined) so as Mark sometimes worked in a threesome he was making a substantial contribution to the interaction. Predictably, the large majority (84 per cent) of Mark's turns in the interaction were gestural or used Makaton signs. For his mainstream school work partners, over one-fifth (23 per cent) of their turns involved using gestures. The length of spoken comments was very short for Mark (one or two morphemes) and longer for his work partners (between one and eleven morphemes, mean 2.9). So in terms of verbal input, Mark was speaking less and saying less when he did speak than was the case for his work partners. He was making up for this with his non-verbal communication.

Mark's limited spoken language makes it difficult to code some of his comments in terms of structure and function. A striking finding is that all Mark's comments received a response from his work partner(s) (see Figure 16). One suspects that this must have been very encouraging for Mark as it was clearly an effort for him to vocalise his thoughts so it would have been important that each effort was recognised. Three-quarters of Mark's comments were a continuation of a topic begun by one of his work partners so he, in turn, was making an effort to respond to them.

Mark's interpretable utterances were divided between monitoring and acknowledgements. There were no clear comments in other categories (see Figure 19).

Mark received a wide variety of types of comment covering the full spectrum of functions. The largest category (38 per cent) was of direct instructions. This was a much higher proportion than was received by either Jane or Tony (see Figures 17 and 18). The comparatively high figure for Mark may reflect the infrequency with which he spoke and therefore his work partners had less explicit information from which to deduce what Mark did, or did not, understand about a task. It is understandable that a reaction to this might be to give more focused instructions. So it is interesting that,

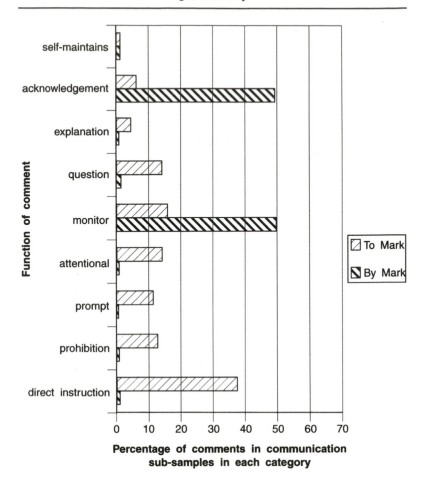

Figure 19 Talk by and to Mark
For key, see notes to Figure 13, page 81

despite this situation, Mark's work partners used many prompts in addition to, or in place of, direct instructions.

Sarah: What's it called?
            ((holding up card leg for the puppet))
Mark: ((grins))
            ((shakes head))
Marie: You do!

	You know!
	[trying to cajole Mark into responding?]
Sarah:	What's it called?
Marie:	What's it called?
Mark:	((looks away))
	((grins))
Marie:	L . . . ?
	((sounding out the first letter))
	L . . . ?
	((bending closer to Mark))
	L . . . ?
	((bending closer to Mark))
Mark:	((half looks at Marie then turns away))
Marie:	It's called a leg!
Mark:	LEG!
Sarah:	**YEH!**

This type of series of prompts was much less usual in talk by Link 7 mainstream school children to work partners from the special school. It is interesting to consider why this was the case. It may be, as noted earlier, that the younger mainstream school children used most of their resources to keep the attention of special school children. Perhaps, beyond that, they could deal only with the immediate task demands, such as instructing the partner which colour to use. These could be formulated second by second as the partner completed each step. Using the type of series of prompts described above required the child guide to hold a clear plan of the task and to compare continually the partner's response against the task. It is likely that the younger mainstream school children lacked the combination of flexibility in both planning and social skills which were needed in this situation. Questions and attentional statements were used often by Mark's work partners and may have been intended to sustain Mark's interest in the shared activity. Taken together these two functional categories accounted for nearly one-third of all talk to Mark.

Mark received some repetitions (just over 4 per cent of all comments) but a very high proportion, compared with classmates, of re-phrasings. Overall, one-sixth of talk to Mark was a re-phrasing of a comment within the speech topic.

Jack

Jack was a 15 year old with one younger (by one year) brother. Jack was reserved and very polite to adults and other pupils. His main interests outside school were sport and his collections of various ephemera. He came from a large, close family and enjoyed visiting his many aunts and uncles. His difficulties were caused by an unspecified illness soon after birth, and he was not taking any medication. He talked infrequently but when he did speak, it was at some length and with a strong urge to communicate. His speech was loud but often difficult to interpret. He worked with both boys and girls from the mainstream school and had no particular favourites among these children but worked amicably with them all.

The proportion of time spent by Jack communicating with his work partners approximately equalled time spent by them communicating with him. For one-quarter of the time Jack was communicating with his work partners and for a further one-third of the time they were communicating with him. There was very little interaction with adults by Jack or his work partners. The remaining time involved the pupils working together, but not communicating, or acting independently.

Analyses of communication turns showed that these were also divided approximately equally between Jack and his work partners. However, whereas one-third of Jack's turns were non-verbal, a very small proportion (6 per cent) of his work partners' turns were solely gestural or speech supported by gesture. Jack's comments were between one and seven morphemes in length (mean 2.7 morphemes), considerably shorter than that of his work partners (range from one to eleven morphemes, mean 4.2). The broad positive correlation between the mean length of comments from the four special school pupils and comments by their work partners (see Figure 20) shows an interesting and consistent relationship between the conversational partners.

Crudely, special school pupils who made only brief comments received brief comments in return, while the opposite also happened. Special school pupils who spoke in comparatively long 'sentences' received longer replies. This points to a possible synchronisation which would be interesting to investigate further to find out what mechanisms prompted it, given that the special

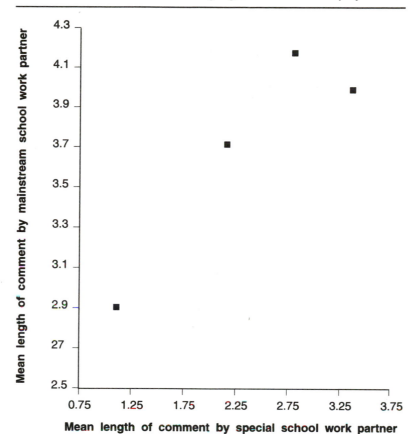

Figure 20 Mean length of comments (in morphemes) between work partners

school pupils provided unusual conversational partners for mainstream school children.

Jack's comments were, of all the target special school pupils, the most strongly integrated with his work partners' talk. Figure 16 shows that over four-fifths of Jack's comments (81 per cent) were a response to his work partners' comments which were in turn followed up by a comment from one of his work partners. In keeping with this, few of Jack's comments introduced new conversational topics that were ignored by his work partners. Like Tony, many of Jack's new topics referred to his experiences or feelings:

Jack: [introducing new topic]

	Half past eight
	Early to school
	Bus came early
	Came at half past ten
	The bus, it did
Suzanna:	Did it?
	[responding to, but not extending, topic or querying the confusion about the time]
Jack:	Yes
	Half past, it did
	Twenty past eight
	Twenty past eight early?
Suzanna:	Yes
	[responding to Jack's question]
Nicola:	((pointing to paper))
	D'you want to put this here?
	[bringing Tony back to the task]

Suzanna's responses acknowledged Jack's comments but did not invite him to expand his ideas. Nicola then returned Jack's attention to the task. The pupils from the mainstream school may have been overconcerned about the task aspects of the sessions. They focused on carrying out and completing activities. This seems to have detracted from developing friendships. If Suzanna and Nicola had been less concerned here with getting on with the task then they may have been more willing to have pursued with Jack the issue, which obviously concerned him, about the bus not arriving on time.

Jack used a wide range of functional strategies (see Figure 21) but about half his talk focused on monitoring what was happening.

A comparatively high proportion, nearly one-third (28 per cent), of Jack's talk was in the form of questions to his work partners. Jack's questions were interesting because he was the only one of the target special school pupils to try to indicate that he or she had not understood a specific word. These pupils were making 'rubbings' and then cutting out sections and gluing these on a large sheet with labels indicating where the rubbing had been made:

Grant:	Can you print that?
	['print' meaning 'write']
Jack:	Print?
Grant:	You can print it there

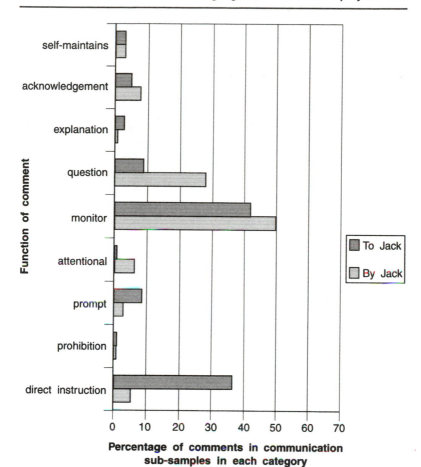

Figure 21 Talk by and to Jack
For key, see notes to Figure 13, page 81

	And then say it was the chair
	[seems to interpret Jack's query as a request for clarification of the whole instruction]
Jack:	Chair?
Grant:	((nodding))
	[offers no clarification]

Jack did not join in the activity after this but just watched. He had not articulated what he did, or did not, understand in sufficient detail for Grant to work out what, if anything, was the problem. Grant appears to have assumed that Jack was able to carry on with the activity. The joint activity seems to have broken down here because neither pupil responded to the linguistic push that was being created by the work partner: Jack to explain his difficulties and Grant to elaborate on the task.

This illustrates the special school pupils' difficulties in making it clear to mainstream school work partners when something had not been understood. Whether these difficulties stemmed from language limitations (i.e. the special school pupil knew he or she had not understood but lacked the linguistic skills to express this) or to a failure to recognise that they had not understood is not clear. On one occasion Jack was more explicit but still not sufficiently so:

Kieran:	You tell us where they go
	[meaning – where to glue shapes]
Jack:	Where?
	Outside or something?
Kieran:	I don't know
	I don't know if we go outside yet

After this there was a brief silence and then Jack watched Kieran. Kieran had not made clear that he still did not understand. Kieran had tried to guess at what Jack meant but this only created mutual confusion in which neither child took the conversational point any further.

Jack was also unusual compared with the other target special school pupils in occasionally articulating his wishes explicitly:

Jeannette:	You write your name first
Jack:	No
	Want you to do yours first
	((handing Jeanette the pencil))
Jeannette:	((writing))

Jack received a wide range of talk from his work partners, dominated by direct instructions and monitoring.

Neither Jack nor his work partners repeated comments within a speech topic. Jack and his work partners re-phrased comments occasionally although this was infrequent overall. Re-phrasing was very infrequent for any of the target special school pupils. This echoes a similar finding by North American researchers who investigated the conversational skills of children with learning difficulties (for example, Bryan *et al.*, 1976; Donahue, 1983). The researchers found that these children did not recognise that it was the job of the speaker to 'repair' a comment if the listener had not understood. Similarly, some research into 'repair' strategies of children with language disorders has found that although these children recognised when a message had not been understood, they were unsystematic in how the comment was revised (Gallagher and Darnton, 1978; McTear and Conti-Ramsden, 1992). Several researchers have found that children with learning difficulties tend to be less influential than other children in directing the course of the task when working in mixed attainment groups (Bryan *et al.*, 1981; Bryan, 1986; Thomson, 1993; see Cohen, 1994, for a review of research into small group interaction).

The Link 11 mainstream school children re-phrased comments to partners slightly less frequently than did mainstream school 7 year olds. This may have been because the older mainstream school children were more astute about commencing an instructional sequence at an appropriate place. The Link 11 mainstream school children, compared with Link 7 mainstream school pupils, gave more explanations (although these were still infrequent) to supplement instructions or monitoring of events and were slightly more inclined to hold back from taking over the task.

CONCLUSION

In both the Link 7 and the Link 11 projects the mainstream school children took on, and developed, roles as guides to special school work partners. The special school pupils responded, in general, positively and, through their responses, made an impact on how the interaction developed. They were not just passive recipients of instructions. There were, however, few occasions on which pupils from the special school could act as guides to mainstream children (discussed further in Chapter 7).

Nevertheless, there were benefits in the interaction for both sets of pupils. Special and mainstream school pupils were, through the link projects, working with pupils who were for the most part very like themselves but who were also, in ways to which our society draws attention, rather different. Inherent in this diversity is the widening of models of language and social interaction.

Special school pupils had direct models of language and social behaviour in classmates which were different from those found in the special schools. Ultimately they may be encouraged to take on more dominant roles in interaction with peers by seeing this demonstrated by children from the mainstream schools. The special school pupils were also pushed into asserting themselves in ways which probably did not happen when they were with teachers or other adults. In that situation the special school pupils would have been more likely to accept the role of tutee whereas they sometimes challenged this when working with a pupil from the mainstream school. It is likely that, through this, the special school pupils were learning how to negotiate roles with peers. These experiences have important implications for the development of autonomy and independence.

The mainstream school children had to draw on a range of linguistic and social strategies to sustain communication with special school work partners. The absence of assumptions about common understandings pushed these children into being more explicit about intentions. This is likely to have prompted, and helped, the mainstream school children to reflect both on the process of carrying out the activity and on their own thinking processes. It is often said colloquially that the best way to learn something is to try to teach it to somebody else. This process was operating much of the time for the mainstream school pupils. Working with pupils who behaved, in some ways, atypically and maybe unpredictably, came at an important time developmentally for these pupils from mainstream schools. The middle years of childhood seem to be a particularly sensitive time for such interactions as it is during this period that children are learning the unwritten rules about being a conversationalist (Robinson and Robinson, 1986).

Chapter 6

End of the year
The impact of link project experiences

What were the views of the children and young people from the special and mainstream schools after a year of link project experiences? Answering that question is the focus of this chapter. Mainstream school children were interviewed individually (Link 7 project) or in small groups of about four children (Link 11 project). (The methodology of interviewing children in groups is discussed in Lewis, 1992.) Views of special school pupils were collected through discussions with both the pupils and their teachers. These views were collected informally and no attempt has been made to quantify them. This chapter includes quotations from the special school pupils.

The views of special school pupils were not collected in a structured way. It would have been valuable to have obtained these views more systematically. This would have required finding a way around the communication difficulties experienced by many pupils, especially those in the Link 7 project. Developments in the use of information technology by people with learning difficulties are likely to make this more feasible in future. Work supported by the National Council for Educational Technology (Detheridge, 1993) is demonstrating the potential of micro-computer technology in allowing children and young people to express what they know but have not been able to communicate. These valuable developments have the potential to give a 'voice' to many individuals whose views have otherwise to be deduced indirectly. If a child shrinks from an approaching stranger but cannot communicate why he or she does this, then someone watching may make a guess about what it is about the situation which appears to cause fear. Similarly, children may appear to enjoy or dislike 'integration' experiences. However, these should not be imposed on the basis of assumptions about the wishes of those involved. Developing inclusion must go alongside endeavours to find ways of unlocking barriers to communication. Then all pupils involved will be able to express a view about the process.

This chapter is in three parts. It begins with a review of the terms in which pupils from the special and mainstream schools described one another. The second part of the chapter looks at what the pupils saw as characterising the school groups to which they belonged. The final section looks at what the mainstream school pupils believed about the causes of severe learning difficulties. From these three elements, it is possible to draw out some developmental trends in children's understanding about the nature of learning difficulties. These have been discussed more fully elsewhere (see Lewis, 1993b).

DESCRIPTIONS OF OTHER CHILDREN AND YOUNG PEOPLE

Physical characteristics in young children's descriptions of others (Link 7 project only)

After a year of joint sessions in the Link 7 project, special and mainstream school children were asked to describe children from the other school. Both sets of children commented mainly on what their work partners looked like (clothes, hair colour, height, etc.). This, as discussed in Chapter 3, is typical of young children's accounts of others. Only one mainstream school child (Liam) commented on the unusual facial appearance of pupils from the special school.

Many of these mainstream school children also described special school work partners as having hearing or visual difficulties. Indeed for some mainstream school children these were the defining characteristics. This was illustrated by two children who described special school pupils as 'handicapped' or 'disabled'. These children went on to say that 'handicapped' or 'disabled' meant not being able to see, hear and/or walk properly. Similar findings have been made by Pamela Maras (1993) in her research comparing the attitudes towards disabled children of non-disabled pupils in segregated, link scheme, and more fully integrated contexts (see Chapter 3).

In the Link 7 project there was no close parallel between disabilities named by the mainstream school children as characterising children from the special school and those children's actual disabilities. For example, all the Link 7 special school pupils experienced speech difficulties but these were identified by only two of the mainstream school children. Hearing aids were worn by only one special school child but hearing impairments were given as a general descriptor by the large majority of the mainstream school children. It is puzzling that children from the special school were so often described as having poor hearing or sight or, less often, physical problems.

There are several possible explanations for why this happened even after a year of working together. First, the mainstream school children may not have recognised any disabilities in special school pupils other than sensory or physical difficulties. These were indicated in ways which could be seen, such as a hearing aid or trembling hands. The hearing aids or powerful lenses may have been assumed to characterise the whole group. This can be summarised as an overgeneralisation of cues, relevant to one or a few individuals, to the whole group. A parallel illustration is of someone who notices a 'young' policeman or woman and then says that all police look 'young'. However, it seems unlikely that the mainstream school children genuinely failed to notice cognitive difficulties of the pupils from the special school. A range of research has shown that children as young as 5 years old quickly deduce where they and classmates stand in terms of relative attainments on school tasks (Crocker and Cheeseman, 1988).

An alternative explanation for why the children from the special school were, incorrectly, described generally as having hearing or visual difficulties is an overinclusive use of those labels. The mainstream school children may have been using labels for disabilities which were understood and so took precedence over poorly understood disabilities. They then de-emphasised the characteristics which did not fit the label. This would explain why attainments of children from the special school, such as reading and spelling, were exaggerated by some mainstream school children. A parallel here is someone who does not recognise systematic differences between bluegrass, country and western, folk and blues music and so calls them all 'country and western'.

Another explanation is that other difficulties were recognised but were thought to be part of sensory or physical impairments. That is, when a child from the special school was described by a child from the mainstream school as 'blind', the mainstream school child may have meant by this that the special school child experienced, for example, both visual and learning difficulties. One child (Alice) consistently and repeatedly linked visual impairments with cognitive difficulties. We might be able to unravel some of this complexity if we could assess what non-disabled children understand about, first, people who have visual impairments but no cognitive difficulties; second, people who have no visual impairments but do have cognitive difficulties; and third, people who have visual impairments and also have cognitive difficulties. It would also be useful to know more about the development of similar concepts held by children with learning difficulties. This is an area about which we currently have little systematic research evidence.

Attainments

Mainstream school children, in both projects, talked about the attainments of special school work partners. In contrast, neither group of special school pupils described mainstream school work partners in terms of what they were able to do on school-related tasks. This may have reflected the dominant ethos of mainstream, contrasted with special, schools. The Link 7 mainstream school children talked about apparent, or presumed, attainments of their special school work partners. Nearly all these comments were phrased positively:

'They do good drawings' (Rachel) (Liam)

'They're good at making pictures' (Andrew)

'They're clever sometimes' (Hamish)

Several of these younger mainstream school children recounted attainments of individual special school children in great detail:

'I done large paintings with Ben and he painted a dish and he painted it but I only done the corners and he painted the rest and he's (. .) good at drawing a picture. I started the grass and sky off and he drawed around and coloured it and all spots and he drawed a picture' (Andrew)

This kind of comment conveyed a sense of shared pride in what the two children had made together. Some similarly detailed accounts seemed to exaggerate what had been achieved:

'Since they've come here they've been ever so good. I like Kirsty. She's still a bit (. .) well, don't know how to put it really (. .) but she's like (. .) she can't work properly on herself . . . I've always worked with Kirsty since she come here so now she's getting ever so good at it (. .) cos she can write. She can spell my name out now and she can say it properly (. .) cos last time when you came [interview near start of project] she couldn't even spell it out (. .) I had to learn her first though . . . When we sing "We're going on a lion hunt" [song taught to all the children by the mainstream school teacher] they're ever so good at singing it. I keep forgetting it so I look at Kirsty and she tells me . . . Kirsty can do, read books by herself, them easy ones, with big [large print] words, I mean little [small print] words, like "This dog is going near the sea".'

[Interviewer – And has she read some of these books to you?]

'Yes she gets them off the shelf. She gets them from over there' (Rachel)

These positive evaluations may have reflected a wish for mainstream school children to say what they thought would be approved. Frances Aboud (1988) has reviewed work concerning attitudes to ethnicity which suggests that social desirability effects emerge after about 7 years old. This may be why ethnic prejudice appears to decline after the early school years (i.e. age 8 upwards).

More positively, constructive evaluations of special school children may also have been a reflection of the optimistic ethos of the project. The teachers deliberately praised children for trying hard. Some of the evaluations of special school work partners, notably Rachel's, were considerably higher than what the children described actually did in school. It is difficult to know how to interpret such apparently genuine overevaluation. Perhaps children like Rachel wanted to see themselves as being helpful and effective with special school work partners and this led to the high evaluations. In some cases apparent overestimation may be due to a difference in interpretation between the child (Rachel here) and an adult's perspective. Rachel's interpretation of 'reading' may have been 'saying the words' so when Kirsty imitated Rachel's reading in this way she was, in Rachel's terms, 'reading the little words'.

Usually, a child's apparent age is a good guide to other children about what to expect that child to be able to do. A particularly interesting and unresearched area is the relationship between non-disabled children's perceptions about hypothesised chronological ages of disabled children and those children's actual ages. The Link 7 mainstream school children underestimated, but only slightly, the ages of their special school work partners. They were thought, after a year of working together, to be between 4 and 7 years old (most mainstream school children said 5 years). This was slightly below those children's actual ages (4 to 8 years) but, interestingly, was little different from estimated ages given near to the start of the Link 7 project. So more prolonged experience of the special school children did not lead to beliefs that they were even younger than had been thought at first. This is surprising in that the special school children were, in developmental terms, at around 2 to 3 years old. In other words, the younger mainstream school children were influenced more by how old the special school children looked than by 'how old' they behaved. None of these mainstream school children made an explicit distinction between chronological and developmental ages of special school work partners.

In contrast to this the Link 11 mainstream school children were not misled by the apparent conflict between ability cues (indicating young age) and physical cues (indicating older age). The 10 and 11 year olds from the mainstream school involved in the Link 11 project could deal with the conflicting sets of age and ability cues. They were clear about explaining this:

'(They have) big bodies, young minds' (Greg)

'Their brains (are) younger than what their bodies are' (Kevin)

'You have to treat them a bit younger than we would ourselves, it seems funny because they're bigger [than us] (Danielle)

'They're about 14 but for a mental age, I'd say about 5' (Ross)

These mainstream school children made relatively accurate guesses about the ages of the special school pupils with whom they worked. The mainstream school children said little about special school pupils' presumed attainments on school tasks. Comments were tied to what had been seen and so based on evidence not guesswork. Assumptions were made about how the special school pupils might feel about their attainments:

'Mark's not all that good at writing, I don't think he enjoys writing but he likes cutting things' (Debbie)

'We talk to Sara [pupil at special school]. She shows us books (. .) we read them to her (. .) she points out the pictures (. .) She likes it then (Grant)

Behaviour

Over three-quarters of Link 7 mainstream school children outlined behaviours of their special school work partners when asked an open-ended question about describing those children. One of the special school pupils occasionally displayed challenging behaviours but, as with references to sensory impairments, misbehaviour was attributed to many of the special school pupils. For over two-thirds of these 6 and 7 year olds who mentioned behaviour, the behaviours were misbehaviours:

'They're naughty' (Samantha)

'They don't do the right things, they just mess about' (Ruth)

'They mess about and you're not supposed to' (Michelle)

'All the boys are a bit too rough . . . Like they run about and you have to go and get them, like they always go in the toilets' (Rachel)

'Emily [Link 7 special school pupil] she sits on the floor and doesn't budge and she's quite heavy and you can't get her up' (Alice)

The misbehaviour made the younger mainstream school children feel uncomfortable and they articulated this in various ways, in particular emphasising that misbehaviour broke classroom rules. A few of the Link 7 mainstream school children tried to explain the reasons for 'naughtiness' by special school children:

'Kirsty tries to eat the plasticene . . . [because] she doesn't know what she can do and what she can't do' (Michelle)

'One little boy, he took his jumper off and then I gave (..)

picked it up and gave it him back and he didn't say "thank you" just grabbed it from me'.
[Interviewer – Why d'you think he didn't say thank you?]
'Cos he don't know how to say it' (Samantha)

When Link 7 mainstream school children were able to articulate a reason for the 'misbehaviour' it was not seen as a deliberate act, but rather the result of lack of information or related to presumed sensory or motor impairments.

'They're not very good at colouring cos they keep going like that [gesturing – drawing over the edge of the paper] and they're not supposed to. They don't do it right'
[Interviewer – So what stops them doing it properly?]
'They don't hold it right' (Carl)

'I don't like it [when they colour in badly] because they spoil the picture and when they did it the first time they came, they put the bead in the paint and Miss Drake [teacher] told them not to
[Interviewer – And did they put it in after that?]
Yes (. .) Because some of them can't hear properly and they didn't hear what she said' (Rachel)

Most of these mainstream school children were sympathetic in their response to misbehaviour:

'It could be that they get fed up of all these things . . . I think they're really happy when they stay at their school. When they're here, they get bored . . . When they're over their school they think it's ever so good cos they know where all [the] things are' (Rachel)

Seven year olds, as is known from much developmental research, are very concerned about rules and keeping to rules. So it is perhaps unsurprising that 'misbehaviour' featured so prominently in these mainstream school children's recollections of link sessions. However, with the exception of Alice, that misbehaviour was seen as an effect, rather than a defining characteristic, of disability. It was not seen as likely to be a permanent feature of special school pupils' classroom lives but a reasonable reaction to the immediate situation.

For the special school children in the Link 7 project, the mainstream school classroom provided an arena in which to test the generalisability of rules known and adhered to in the special school. None of the children from the special school, in discussions about the link project, commented on their own or other children's classroom behaviour. Sheenagh Hardie's autobiographical account of living with Down's syndrome shows that, in a similar situation, she was aware of the impact of her behaviour on other children:

> Any kiddies I used to enjoy playing with would sometimes shun me. Maybe that was because I would play rough, pushing and punching at times – but I didn't really understand . . .. We Down's imitate what we see and I was just copying what I'd seen other kiddies doing.
>
> (1991: 15)

References to misbehaviour may give the erroneous impression that pupils, especially those from the special school, were often 'naughty' in the Link 7 classroom. Systematic and structured observational data collected during the Link 7 project showed that misbehaviours by any child were infrequent. It was the salience, not the frequency, of misbehaviour which made a strong impact on many of the mainstream school children.

It is predictable, given developmental differences, that perceived misbehaviour of special school work partners was not an issue for the older mainstream school children involved in the Link 11 project. These children made few references to misbehaviour of special school work partners. This no doubt reflected the greater maturity of both groups of children. Ten and 11 year olds tend to be less concerned with rule keeping than are 6 and 7 year olds. Also, the Link 11 special school pupils were familiar with school expectations whereas the special school children involved in the Link 7 project were still learning about appropriate classroom rules and behaviour. Link 11 mainstream school pupils did talk about what caused odd behaviours of special school work partners. These mainstream school pupils seemed to regard special school pupils' unusual behaviours as curious but, in those pupils' terms, logical responses to the situation. Whereas the younger mainstream school children saw 'unusual' behaviours as rule breaking, the older children were less upset by these and clear about the appropriate reaction:

'Sara makes a lot of noise. She does that to get attention . . .
That's why you have to tell her off' (Janine)

'They just like attention. Some of them . . . I mean if they look
like . . . they just look at you and they keep on looking around
and then they . . . you just keep on talking to them . . . they
just like attention' (Ross)

It is not possible to know from where these 10 and 11 year old
mainstream school children drew these conclusions. They may
have been told such things explicitly by adults or may have reached
these judgements themselves. There was one aspect of special
school work partners' behaviour which was discussed at length by
their work partners from the mainstream school in the Link 11
project. This arose spontaneously in all the small discussion groups
and concerned the pushing, hugging and kissing which some
special school pupils (particularly Mark) directed at some mainstream school children. The following extract is from one of the
small discussion groups of four girls from the mainstream school:

Sarah: I don't think Mark will stop kissing you
Marnie: He's always kissing me and Frankie and other people
              as well
Interviewer: Do you like that?
Marnie: Well (. .) some people are afraid to say 'No stop it'
              they just let it (. .) it happening but they just (. .)
              they're afraid to say 'No stop it'
Interviewer
[to Frankie]: Do you like it? Cos Mark's your special friend isn't he?
Frankie: Yes. I don't like it sometimes
Sarah: Bit embarassing
Marnie: Yes it's embarassing. I've had loads of people kept
              saying WHOOOO and everything like that. And
              then (. .) it's (. .) um (. .) he's (. .) he can be pretty rough
              though
Catherine: Yeh
Marnie: He can (. .) Like when we were in the playground he
              chased the girls ROUND AND ROUND AND
              ROUND AND ROUND AND ROUND and eventu-
              ally he gets dizzy

These girls extended one another's contributions, perhaps reveal-
ing more about their feelings of embarrassment than would have

been the case if they had talked alone with the interviewer. The behaviours which they described were typical of Mark's actions and seem to have created some ambivalence in many of the mainstream school children. While they liked Mark's friendliness this sometimes became too rough. They did not like this but some felt unable to stop it.

The young people from the special school involved in the Link 11 project made very few comments about classroom behaviour apart from some general remarks about working hard, for example 'Me and Greg, we work hard we do' (Tony).

Abstract qualities

The younger children (special and mainstream school) made very few unprompted references to psychological attributes of special school work partners. In contrast, these references were very commmon in the older pupils' (special and mainstream school) descriptions of one another. This is consistent with what we know about children's changing descriptions of other people (reviewed in Chapter 3). The most frequent descriptors used by the Link 11 mainstream school children about young people from the special school concerned personality, especially their cheerfulness and friendliness:

'They're [young people from special school] good at making other people feel good' (Michael)

'They make us feel welcome' (Greg)

'You don't often see them sad' (Cora)

'They smile all the time . . . You don't often see them sad or anything . . . They love to talk and they love to make friends with you . . . They're not shy or anything' (Roger)

'They love to talk and they love to make friends with you' (Marie)

'They are very happy, very happy with us . . . and um some of them laugh quite a lot and like (. .) many of them (. .) they're peaceful and kind' (Janine)

'They try hard' (Sunny)

One child drew attention to the humour of some special school pupils:

> 'There's this one guy – Tony – who I work with and whenever we have any spare time he always says 'Come on guv, let's draw a picture!' (Kevin)

Although the mainstream school children's descriptions of the special school pupils may sound stereotypical, reminiscent of the 'happy-go-lucky-Down's' stereotype, it is important to note that the same kinds of qualities were given by special school pupils when describing mainstream school children:

> 'They're my friends' (Kim)

> '(They're?) good fun' (Jack)

> '(They tell?) good jokes' (Tony)

Thinking processes

A marked contrast between the two age groups of mainstream school children concerned the extent to which they were able to imagine how their special school work partners thought about the world. The older mainstream school children talked about this a great deal. However, only one of the Link 7 mainstream school pupils (Alice) made any comments about the hypothesised thinking processes of the children with whom she worked from the special school. Alice explained what she saw as the difficulties of her special school work partners as due to brain malfunction:

> 'Her brain tells her ears to do the wrong thing . . . Yes and their brain tells them the wrong thing, because it forgets the message . . . They want to get better at things so they can be like us . . . They want to be like other people that can do things'

This account may have been prompted by the teachers' explanation for the Link 7 special school children's behaviour – that the children's brains were like a LEGO model with a piece missing. None of the other Link 7 mainstream school children with whom the nature of learning difficulties was discussed made any reference to this point. The ways in which teachers explain disability and activities for fostering inclusion were discussed in Chapter 3.

It is becoming increasingly clear that being able to think about one's own thinking processes, and to extend this to conjecture about others' thinking processes, is a very important step developmentally (see work on the 'theory of mind': Leslie, 1987; Astington *et al.*, 1988; Perner, 1991). Older poor readers have been shown to improve their reading if they:

- articulate how they are tackling the task,
- consider which strategies seem to be working, and
- reflect on why these strategies seem to work, for example '"The cat sat on the _? _" don't know that word, look at the first letter "c", have a guess, "car" no doesn't make sense, . . .'

(These areas are reviewed in Raban and Lewis, 1994). Extrapolating from this, a valuable spin-off from the link projects may have been in fostering pupils' metacognitive skills. The nature of the activities prompted pupils to articulate how they would tackle tasks and sometimes to defend their strategies. For the mainstream school children, thinking this through also seems to have prompted them to think about how their special school work partners would approach the activity. This happened through tutoring and also through discussions after link sessions. Both groups of pupils routinely discussed events in the link sessions with adults and other children.

The older mainstream school children made guesses about how the world views of special school work partners compared with those of mainstream school children. This seemed to fascinate the mainstream school children:

> 'Marie [pupil from special school] is ever so shy. She's really quiet and shy. One of my friends (. .) well, she thinks she can't talk. But I don't think (. .) I think she's too shy, she thinks um (. .) that no one will like her if she starts talking all the time so she's always quiet . . . and you have to (. .) we got pretty friendly with her' (Hannah)

Hannah had come to her own conclusions about the reasons for Marie's quietness. These reasons differed from those put forward by a mainstream school friend who, reminiscent of the younger mainstream school children's explanations, reportedly attributed lack of speech to a physical impairment.

In all the small discussion groups with 10 and 11 year olds from the mainstream school there were lengthy discussions, initiated by the children, about how the special school pupils might feel about the mainstream school children. This generated intense debate about how much the special school pupils understood about their own, and others', cognitions. A particular issue was whether or not the special school pupils thought themselves to be like pupils in mainstream schools. A fuller account of comments by three different children illustrates the range of nuances encompassed by these statements. Siobhan's comment implied that she saw the mainstream school children as having different capabilities from the special school pupils but that this difference was not perceived by the special school pupils.

'They don't seem to know what they're missing' (Siobhan)

Greg's comment implied that the special school pupils were thought both to recognise and resent the differences between their and mainstream school pupils' capabilities.

'Inside they've got their own qualities (but) they must feel angry that they can't do what we can do' (Greg)

Greg's comment implied that mainstream school pupils had greater capabilities than did special school pupils. This was not the case in the latter part of Janine and Michael's comments:

'They [special school pupils] might [if in a mainstream school] realise that they weren't the same cos they wouldn't be able to do what we would be able to do. When they're with other people [at the special school] they're the same aren't they? They probably think we're the weird ones . . . They probably think we're the weird ones cos we know things like 10 add 10'

Janine, whose ideas were later picked up by Michael, perceived a difference between special and mainstream school pupils. She thought that the special school pupils also perceived this difference. The difference did not assume superiority of special or mainstream school pupils. Janine made a complex conceptual leap and recognised that two actors in a situation not only see things from different points of view but may understand, speculate on, and reject, the other's point of view. She could apply this to her classmates, contrasted with a relatively unfamiliar group – pupils from a special school. Janine was the only child to articulate this degree of conceptual complexity when speculating about the thought processes of the special school work partners.

These mainstream school children had great difficulty in working out whether the special school pupils who had started life as non-disabled would know this:

'If they were born like it, they wouldn't know; if they had a car crash when they were ten or something, then they'd realise' (Kevin)

Kevin seemed unable to conceive of memory as reversible; that is, that a child might develop a normal memory and then lose it. Some of these mainstream school children were genuinely puzzled about what special school pupils knew about their own cognitions:

'Don't they know that they can't do everything that everyone else can?' (Greg)

Michael replied:

'No, because the teachers treat them [Link 11 special school pupils] normally just like anyone else that comes in the room'

Michael's answer to Greg shows that he made an implicit connection between teachers' treatment of pupils and pupils' self-concepts.

None of the special school pupils talked in similar ways about their own, or others', thinking processes. A more structured approach to eliciting their views might have generated comments about this. There is a dearth of research evidence about these kinds of metacognitive skills in people with learning difficulties.

SAME OR DIFFERENT? INTER-GROUP RELATIONS

In general, children from special schools were seen, by the Link 7 mainstream school children, as different from mainstream school children although this was not a clear cut division. Special school children had some distinguishing characteristics (such as presumed sensory or motor impairments) which differentiated them from mainstream school children. In other ways (for example, preferred activities, classroom rules) they were seen as similar to mainstream school children. Similarity, in terms of being subject to the same classroom rules, was reinforced by teachers' messages to the mainstream school children about not doing too much for children from the special school:

'They work ever so hard when they're over here (. .) cos (. .) if
Mr Willow sees them being naughty he'll tell them off like he
should do cos if he don't tell them off they'll keep doing it (. .)
and don't know what they're doing' (Rachel)

The special school children were seen as needing some, but not
extensive, help. Successful inclusive policies are likely to lead to an
avoidance of non-disabled children giving too much, or inappropriate, help to disabled children. Complementing this, schools
promoting an inclusive ethos may explicitly encourage disabled
children to help the non-disabled, when appropriate. Several of
these young mainstream school children gave examples of ways in
which special school children had helped them (as in Rachel's
earlier reference to Kirsty helping her to learn the words of the
'Going on a Lion Hunt' song).

'They [special school children] help our [mainstream school]
children (. . . .) (And) when they come we help them, so
they're getting good at things so now they can help us'
(Michelle)

They reiterated teachers' instructions not to do too much for special
school pupils, thus emphasising similarities across the groups,
mutual support and avoidance of learned helplessness in the
special school children:

'We help them a little bit (. .) just (. .) but not too much else
they'll never learn to do it themselves' (Samantha)

While the Link 7 mainstream school children seemed to have
understood the spirit of the message, and would echo it as a 'rule',
they sometimes had difficulty operating it. There was a tension
between what they understood to be the expectation of equality
and implementing that expectation.

The Link 11 mainstream school children made more references
to differences within the special school group than did the younger
mainstream school children. This suggests that they were not
responding purely by giving what were presumed to be socially
desirable characteristics of special school pupils ('They're all very
happy' type of response).

Some of these older mainstream school children also described
strong similarities between special and mainstream school children:

'They've got exactly the same level of ability as we have when they want to use energy . . . I think they have got just about the same . . . the same ability as we've got . . . I think they can do more or less anything we can do' (Roger)

'They like attention (. .) and they like to play (. .) just like normal children really' (Kevin)

Teachers' attempts to treat special school pupils 'normally' was a cause of confusion for some of these older mainstream school children:

'The teachers tell you not to . . . make them . . . the teachers tell you . . . the teachers tell you treat them like yourself but you can't really . . . cos they tell you to let them paint and everything and then they do it all WRONG and everything' (Kathy)

This comment was greeted with enthusiastic agreement from other mainstream school children in the small discussion group. Kathy seemed to have articulated something which was a difficulty for many of these mainstream school children. Teachers appeared to be denying patently evident differences. This left the mainstream school children puzzled about appropriate behaviour with special school pupils. The message they had been given was one of not drawing attention to differences between special and mainstream school pupils but when they tried to take this message literally, and base interactions with special school work partners on this, then the interaction could not be sustained. Perhaps Kathy's comment reveals a confusion among adults about whether the disabled are like the non-disabled. Should we ignore differences (as implied in the teachers' reported views) or recognise and celebrate difference? It is a much debated issue at all levels and crystallised in opposing responses to charity fund raising on behalf of disabled people.

Projected adult lives

After only two link sessions the Link 7 mainstream school children said that the special school pupils were likely to have the same kinds of adult lives as would mainstream school children. (The results of these early interviews are not reported in detail here.) This view was largely unchanged after a year of link sessions. At that time three-quarters of these mainstream school children stated unequivocally that the special and mainstream school children would have similar jobs. These included work as teachers, taxi drivers, cleaners, gardeners, playgroup leaders, shop workers and milkmen. Special and mainstream school children were also seen as likely to have similar personal lives. These included being married with children, living in flats or houses, shopping, gardening and seeing family or friends at weekends. Perhaps this reflected the mainstream school children's egocentricity. They reflected their own lives onto those of others. However, if this was so, then it indicates that any perception of difference was not so great as to dislodge this egocentricity. A minority of the mainstream school children said that the special school children would not be capable of carrying out a job (paid work or managing a home).

Almost identical predictions about the future lives of special school work partners were given by mainstream school 10 and 11 year olds in the Link 11 project. Predictions were similarly positive, tending to over- rather than to underestimate what might be achieved. This may have reflected the messages from teachers, reported by Kathy (above), emphasising similarity of special and mainstream school pupils. Some of the special school pupils went on work experience placements and these had been a topic of conversation among pupils and adults in the link sessions. This talk seemed to have had a big influence on the mainstream school children's ideas about likely adult lives of special school pupils. In discussion, the older mainstream school children often backed up an idea about types of job for special school pupils by referring to what they had heard about work experience.

When the special school pupils talked about their own wishes for the future they reflected the same kinds of predictions as made by the mainstream school children:

'(I'll?) have a flat' (Tony)

'(I'm going to?) make things and have a boyfriend' (Jane)

Special friends

Neither link project involved the explicit allocation of 'special friends' in link sessions. However, after a year of link sessions all except one of the Link 7 mainstream school children claimed to have a best friend among the special school group. All these mainstream school children said that they would like to play with this friend at playtime (recess). As the link sessions did not include a playtime it was not possible to see whether this happened. Friendships with special school children often reflected a sense of reciprocity:

'She likes me, so I like her. When I first had her she seemed to be kind to me and when I didn't want to hold her hand, she just wanted to hold it. So I holded her hand' (Michelle)

Integration

Most of the Link 7 mainstream school children were positive about the idea of fuller integration into their classes of special school children. The minority of mainstream school children who did express reservations commented on potential practical problems, like a lack of chairs or not enough reading books. About half the mainstream school children would like to have had the special school children visit their homes. Reservations concerned practicalities:

'I would [like Emily to stay] but I don't know where she would sleep' (Michelle)

or fears that the special school children would be messy and cause parental disapproval:

'They might throw the food about and my mum'd be cross' (Steve)

Older mainstream school children were, like the younger mainstream school children in the Link 7 project, generally supportive of greater integration. Special school pupils were seen as being able to do the same kinds of activities as done by mainstream school children with some differentiation:

'If they came in maths they could do something else . . . We don't often get maths the whole lesson . . . You have something on the board or just a page to do and then when you've done that page or um the maths on the board you just finish things off . . . So it'd be all right if they came' (Debbie)

'It's be good . . . They're nice. I was a bit frightened of them at first when I first met them (. .) cos like they make noises but I got used to it and it's really nice now. I think most of the things they can do' (Nicola)

Hannah and Jeannete talked together about what they would do if one of the girls from the special school joined their mainstream school:

Hannah: 'If Sandy [girl from special school] came we would try and be friendly and encourage her and things like that (. .) And do more things (. .) and ask her more questions

Jeanette: mm and ask her what she likes and talk to her a lot and like play

Hannah: And say 'Do you like it?' 'Do you like to do this and that?'

Jeanette: And when we're actually doing things say 'Which colour would you like' or things like that

Hannah: That's what I (. .) we find they like doing (. .) I know some of them they don't like doing that (. .) some of the older ones don't want to be asked they ask you to choose which colour but Sandy (. .) she likes to choose

None of the Link 11 mainstream school pupils cited aggressive or other negative behaviours by mainstream school children, or violent or unpredictable behaviours by special pupils as factors in reservations about fuller integration. These have been mentioned by some pupils in a study of older children's (in a segregated mainstream school) attitudes towards integration (Kyle and Davies, 1991).

However, some of the Link 11 mainstream school children did have reservations about further integration. These reservations reflected responsibilities for special school pupils:

'You'd have to look after them most of the time they're there' (Ben)

and reservations about mainstream school life being too difficult for special school children:

Robert: 'They might get teased (. .) They might get teased, you know, how they look, how they speak, how they – a few things. Some of them run a bit funny

Hannah: (But) it would be good for us to learn how to work
              with handicapped people (. .) fun

Some of the older mainstream school children had reservations
about playtime (recess/break) rather than the classroom and,
interestingly, echoed the MLD school children's reported reservations about mainstream schools (see Chapter 2).

Greg: It's good at their playground cos they've like got
              things to climb on so they've got lots to do
Interviewer: And you haven't got those sorts of things in your
              playground?
Michael: No we're not allowed
Janine: We've got the infant climbing frame but we're not
              allowed on that
Kathy: We're not allowed but they have got concrete under-
              neath so if they fell off they would hurt themselves
Michael: But there [special school] they've got this kind of (. .)
Greg: mat
Michael: Kind of mat stuff like they have at Penny Park which
              is (. .) soft

The special school pupils in the Link 7 and Link 11 projects were
not asked whether they would prefer to attend special or mainstream schools. All those able to communicate a view and who
chose to do so were very positive about their current schools.

CAUSES OF ABILITY/DISABILITY

Mainstream school children talked about causes of ability and
disability. These did not arise in any comments by special school
pupils.

When Link 7 mainstream school children were given information about their special school work partners this had referred to
their 'brains not working quite right'. The mainstream school
children had not been alerted to sensory impairments but it was
cues about these which seem to have been noticed and overgener-
alised.

For many of the Link 7 mainstream school children, special
school children were seen as 'normal but young' and likely to grow
out of what seemed to be temporary difficulties. For others, learning difficulties, as discussed earlier, were subsumed under, or

overridden by, presumed sensory or physical impairments. Their misunderstandings about the nature of severe learning difficulties were evident in confusions about permanent and transient characteristics of the special school children. Sickness or being poorly, which were mentioned by a few Link 7 mainstream school children as causes of learning difficulties after brief contact with their special school work partners, were not mentioned at all at the end of the year. This was possibly because the special school children appeared to have failed to 'get better'. It may be that the mainstream school children could not envisage children having long term illness and so remaining 'poorly' for the whole year. It also suggests that negative messsages about disability as sickness had not been reinforced during the year.

Home factors were sometimes seen as underlying the differences between special and mainstream school children:

'He doesn't eat the right stuff at home' (Steve)

'His mum was poorly when he was born' (Liam)

'They haven't got no mums or dads' (Carl)

'They could have got under their dad's or their mum's feet ... so they could have pushed them and they could have fell or something' (Samantha)

'The mum didn't teach him at home' (Rachel)

None of the special school children were seen as responsible for their special needs. This was in marked contrast to attitudes towards mainstream school classmates with difficulties who were seen much less sympathetically. They were regarded as responsible for their poor attainments in school which were usually seen to be a result of not trying hard enough or misbehaving. The overall picture of these classmates with mild learning difficulties was of children who were not well liked, wilfully misbehaved and therefore caused their own difficulties. The following examples give a flavour of the type of responses made by 6 and 7 year old mainstream school children to the question, 'Why are they "not very clever" [mainstream school classmates named earlier by the child interviewed], children like that?'

'They miss school' (Michelle)

'They don't take their books home' (Alice)

'They don't do what the teacher says' (Samantha)

'They're always doing stuff they shouldn't be doing' (Steve)

'They're naughty' (Andrew) (Michelle)

'They talk and it's not allowed' (Ruth)

'They don't try' (Rachel)

In keeping with these explanations 'not very clever' classmates were generally seen as able to become clever if, and when, they decided to do so.

The Link 11 children from the mainstream school had broadly accurate ideas about the nature of learning difficulties. However, despite abilities to deal with the conflicting age / capability cues and the apparent complexity of some of these children's ideas, they were still confused about some aspects of disability. This emerged, most revealingly, in a discussion among a group of these mainstream school children about their school piano tuner:

Cora:	There's a man what comes in and tunes our piano – he's blind
Bobbie:	He's deaf
Ross:	He's blind
Cora:	He's both
Greg:	He's not deaf. That's why (. .) that's why he's a piano tuner you see (. .) cos if you're blind you can see better
Cora:	Eh?
Ross:	Yeh he's blind, not deaf though . . . If he was deaf he couldn't tune the piano – he wouldn't be able to hear it

CONCLUSION

Overwhelmingly, special and mainstream school pupils at both age groups reported that they found the link sessions fun, they had made new friends and wanted the sessions to continue. This was illustrated in mainstream school children's expressed willingness to work and play with pupils from special schools. Reservations about integration were predominantly pragmatic (for the younger mainstream school children), empathetic (for example, worries about how the pupils would cope) or reflecting concerns about their own degree of responsibility for special school work partners (for the older mainstream school children).

It cannot be claimed that any of these views were directly attributable to the link projects as we do not know in detail what else was happening to the children (special and mainstream school) over the year. For example, a child's views may have changed through attendance at an integrated 'Brownies' pack. Even if the link projects led directly to changes of view and, both intuitively and from other research, one would expect this to be the case, we cannot say with certainty which elements of the link projects caused these changes. For example, it may not have been contact with pupils from the other type of school which led to changed views. Teacher attitudes may have changed and these attitudes permeated many aspects of classroom life, leading to children's revised views. There are also important developmental considerations. For the 7-year-old mainstream school children, in particular, the pace of social and emotional development may have led to altered views after a year, regardless of the nature or existence of specific intervention.

Non-disabled children, and adults, hold many misconceptions about the nature of learning difficulties. The abstract nature of these difficulties makes them particularly difficult for young children to understand. The Link 7 mainstream school children confused learning difficulties with, in the short term, sickness, and in the longer term, sensory or motor impairment. By age 11 mainstream school children had a much clearer understanding of the nature of learning difficulties. They recognised that learning difficulties were neither a sickness nor necessarily related to sensory impairment. They were essentially permanent but this did not lead the children interviewed to place low expectations on likely futures of known young people with special needs. Mainstream school 11, but not 7, year olds could cope with the apparently conflicting sets of cues in classmates with learning difficulties. This led some of the older mainstream school children to describe special school pupils as having young minds in old bodies. However, even at age 11, relatively familiar and well-understood disabilities such as hearing impairment seemed to exert a halo effect on the understanding of other disabilities. Overall, there was a shift across the two mainstream school age groups in spontaneous descriptions of special school work partners. The shift was from emphasising sensory and motor characteristics to emphasising abstract, especially personality, attributes.

The link projects embodied many features associated with positive attitude change. These features included structured working, collaborative working and a positive ethos. The following chapter extends the implications for policy and practice of findings from the projects discussed in previous chapters.

Chapter 7

Conclusions and implications

Schools need to recognise and build on the strengths of enabling pupils like Hamish and Jane (discussed in Chapters 4 and 5 respectively) but also to support children like Alice (see Chapter 4) without sacrificing other pupils' interests. To do so effectively requires both a strong commitment to promoting an inclusive ethos and the means to realise that commitment. This chapter synthesises the implications from the various research projects discussed in earlier chapters. Seven themes emerged: the pros and cons of visitor status, balancing of guide and partner roles, the communication push, barriers to communication, respect for individuals, adults' responses to 'misbehaviour', and the importance of monitoring interaction.

VISITOR STATUS – PART WAY TO INCLUSION?

In both link projects some pupils were visitors to the other school. In this sense the context, and possibly interactions, in the link projects may have been very different from those to be found in schools operating an inclusive ethos. However, this 'partial integration' is, as outlined in Chapter 1, found in many countries. Sometimes it is an end in itself; sometimes it is a step towards inclusion. The visitor status of special school children in the Link 7 project and mainstream school pupils in the Link 11 project may have exaggerated group differences and, contrary to what one might expect, that separateness may have encouraged positive attitudes (see Maras, 1993).

A mismatch between acceptance of visiting pupils compared with full-time classmates was reflected in a comment by one of the teachers. A teacher from one of the mainstream schools wrote in her diary of the link project:

> 'I wish my [mainstream school] children could accept behaviour problems of their peers in the way that they accept the behaviour of [special school] children. [It's] difficult because although I do talk to [mainstream school] children about their own behaviour and why they are actually doing things it is another matter to explain this to a class.

It is possible that the visitor status of one group of pupils limited the generalisability of attitude changes. For example, more sympathetic views of pupils from special schools may not have been generalised to classmates with difficulties because those two groups were seen as qualitatively different. Similarly, pupils from the special school may not have generalised positive attitudes about mainstream pupils to children from other mainstream schools. An inclusive ethos would, by definition, stress the need for sympathetic and positive responses to anyone with any sort of difficulties or difference.

'Visitor status' encouraged special and mainstream school staff to plan collaboratively and to work together in the classroom. Through this process staff, parents and children moved from a segregated system towards a more inclusive approach. The value of this was shown not just in staff directly involved but also in changes of attitude in many of the mainstream school staff who were not involved in the projects. Many of these teachers were initially apprehensive about the projects but subsequently included some of the special school pupils in their classes full time or on regular, individual placements.

The link projects increased the range of resources that became available to each school group. Mainstream school pupils gained access to specialist resources, such as soft play rooms and multisensory environments, which they would not otherwise have experienced. These may be prohibitively expensive to provide in every school even in a totally inclusive system. Special school pupils could use a wider range of classroom resources than found within individual special schools. All groups of pupils gained access to a greater diversity of micro-computer software and peripherals than were found in the separate schools. This differentiation of school resources was a source of pride and enjoyment to pupils from each school. This was particularly evident in the comments of children attending segregated special schools for pupils with moderate learning difficulties who spoke proudly of the envy of neighbourhood friends who did not have schools with, for example, soft play areas.

Controversially, the large number of pupils from the special school who went together into the mainstream school in the Link 7 project may be seen as a way of fostering those children's cultural identity. This contentious point is elaborated well by Micheline Mason:

> There is a particular danger in attempting to integrate individuals or a very small group of disabled children into a large, well-established non-disabled community of children and staff in that there may be no attempt to foster positive and collective identity as young disabled people within an integrated setting, as people see this as a reactionary step.
>
> (1990: 28)

STRUCTURE: BALANCING ROLES

In Chapter 3 the importance of structure in link sessions was discussed. There is an inherent inequality between pupils if joint activities invariably require one pupil (or group of pupils) to take the lead over others. Despite teachers' best intentions this tended to happen in these link projects. Mainstream school children were inclined to dominate the activities, especially at the younger age group. This is predictable in terms of the developmental characteristics of young children. However, it creates a danger that special school pupils may develop learned helplessness.

Such inequalities could have been reduced in the link projects if more of the tasks had genuinely involved the special school pupils acting as guides to mainstream school pupils. There are two main ways in which this could have been done: first, by focusing on tasks with which special but not mainstream school pupils were familiar. These tasks might have included learning Makaton sign language, horse riding or using particular micro-computer programs. There may also have been games and songs known by special school pupils, but not by their mainstream school work partners, which they could have taught. Special school pupils would have been more likely to have taken the lead naturally in these activities. If this had been the case then there would probably have been fewer overall differences in the types of language strategy used by special and mainstream school pupils (i.e. special school pupils would have been equally directive). Thus their language use would have been broadened. Children with learning difficulties may need to be encouraged to be leaders in interactions with other pupils, for example by asking questions of the other child, and extending the conversation topic. Developing these requires social skills and self-confidence as well as linguistic abilities. These pupils must see themselves as having something worth communicating, and as being worth communicating with, if they are to be effective conversational partners with other pupils.

A second strategy to counter the inherent dominance of the more skilled work partner would have been to group children more closely by developmental, not chronological, levels. In the Link 7 project the two groups of children were of the same chronological age but differed widely developmentally. There has been much debate about whether age or developmental level should be the main basis for grouping pupils. The findings from this research suggest that for at least some of the time, similar developmental levels (across special/mainstream school divides) should be the basis for grouping. This will be more feasible within broad primary or secondary age phases. For example, it may be reasonable for a 10 year old with severe learning difficulties to work for part of the time with non-disabled 7 year olds (if this is developmentally appropriate) but a policy of developmental matching could lead to inappropriate placements. It may be undesirable (on social and emotional grounds) for a 14 year old with severe learning difficulties to work with non-disabled 6 year olds.

Interestingly in the Link 11 project there was a closer developmental match between special and mainstream school pupils in that they were not of the same chronological ages. The special school pupils were between one and four years older than the mainstream school children. This may have been a contributory factor in the ease with which those two groups worked together. It was reflected strongly in some of the exchanges which developed around the fringes of the sessions, for example as pupils cleared away. One young man from the special school asked a boy from the mainstream school if he liked doing sums. The two pupils discovered a shared enthusiasm and began to leave one another pages of sums to complete before the next session. This happened independently of the adults and was sustained with great enthusiasm over several weeks. Such interactions form the basis for friend-ships rather than tutoring. Thus broad developmental matching of pupils when working together, opportunities to foster common interests and careful selection of activities so that all pupils get the chance to take on guide and partner roles are important in fostering positive interaction.

THE COMMUNICATION PUSH

A strong finding from both link projects was of the capabilities of the children and young people in working together. The teacher diaries recorded many instances of pupils (special and mainstream school, at both age groups) exceeding expectations. In general, pupils rose to the challenges of the novel context rather than being daunted by them. In particular, they rose to the challenges presented in relation to trying to communicate effectively with one another. This was particularly so for the 6 and 7 year olds from the mainstream school involved in the Link 7 project. These children did not readily abandon attempts to communicate with special school work partners. On one occasion one of these mainstream school children re-phrased a comment nine times successively in an attempt to get her message across. This persistence may have been overenthusiastic. Special school work partners may have welcomed a respite from these well-meaning attempts. An ethos which recognises and promotes respect for individuals can curb a healthy desire to communicate which may become a burden on the recipient.

The language data from the link projects showed how both special and mainstream school pupils provided a linguistic push, prompting work partners to use what were probably relatively undeveloped linguistic strategies. This applied to special school pupils trying to communicate with mainstream school children and to mainstream school children trying to communicate with special school work partners. Each presented the other with un-usual, perhaps unique, linguistic and social demands. A different, more experimental, type of research would be needed to demon-strate a direct and explicit link between language gains and interactions with unusual conversationalists.

How was the situation unusual for the special school pupils? They were with mainstream school children who were unused to them and so lacked the experience from which to guess easily what special school pupils were communicating. These special school pupils were used to being around other pupils and adults who had come to know their communication styles and strategies. This was not the case when those special school pupils addressed children (or adults) from the mainstream school. There, the special school pupils were less readily understood and so were likely to have had to work harder at communicating than would otherwise have been the case.

The link projects also meant that special school pupils had close contact with children who, compared with classmates, provided relatively advanced language models. Adults from the special schools involved in the projects reported examples of special school pupils repeating language structures which they had heard used by mainstream school work partners. Special school pupils did this outside link sessions, suggesting that they were learning, not just to imitate immediately mainstream school children's talk, but also to use these phrases appropriately later. This is anecdotal evidence but indicates that such claims would be worth following up more systematically.

Some of the special school pupils involved in the link projects were markedly and, according to their teachers, unusually self-assertive when working with mainstream school children. Roles had to be negotiated because the context was new and unusual for both groups of pupils. The comparatively high numbers of adults in segregated special school classrooms meant that special school pupils were used to having adults around who would protect their interests if these were threatened by other pupils. This can be an important safeguard for vulnerable children but may also lead to an overprotectiveness. In the link sessions special school pupils sometimes actively resisted mainstream school children's dominance of the interaction. Assertiveness towards peers in socially acceptable ways is an important social skill but one which was less likely to be called upon amid the relatively high adult–pupil ratio of segregated special schools. The link sessions provided a safe environment in which to develop and practise such social skills with classmates.

How was the situation unusual for mainstream school children? For them, there were many instances in which they experimented with ways of re-phrasing comments to special school work partners. This was more apparent with the younger mainstream school children, who were experimenting with taking account of the listener's apparent needs, than with the older mainstream school children who had matured into competent conversationalists. Developmental research suggests that children's ability to adjust talk to the perceived needs of the listener develops during middle childhood (approximately 8 to 11 years). One thing which elicits these abilities is an obvious cue from the listener that the message has not been understood. Work partners who, as listeners, lose concentration quickly, appear to understand only part of what is said to them. They are generally at comparatively early developmental levels and prompt speakers to be clearer about what they are trying to communicate. These were features which characterised many of the special school pupils.

The intriguing synchrony between special and mainstream school pupils in the Link 11 project in terms of the length of individual comments suggests that the mainstream school pupils were tuning into special school pupils' linguistic needs. Whatever the mechanism, the outcome was that special school pupils who said relatively little when it was their turn to speak, received and/or were responding to comparatively short responses in return. At both age groups, mainstream school pupils were, in general, making appropriate deductions about the level and style of language which would be understood by special school work partners.

BARRIERS TO COMMUNICATION

The developmental patterns of the non-disabled children and the characteristics of the talk of pupils with severe learning difficulties conspired to foster the verbal domination of the mainstream school children. Yet, this is clearly only a partial picture of the interaction in the link projects. The pupils were, to some extent, using different forms of communication. To communicate successfully all the children needed to be 'bilingual'. This required pupils to learn and practise supplementary methods of communication; 'supplementary' being signing for mainstream school children and spoken language for special school pupils.

There were some specific aspects of the interaction between special and mainstream school pupils which hampered constructive communication but which could have been remedied. For example, mainstream school children were often either confused about, or failed to use, sign language and sometimes signed to the back of a special school child. To adults, the fact that signing has to be seen by the 'listener' was probably thought to be too obvious to mention and yet, for the younger mainstream school children, not realising this brought to a halt what should have been a successful piece of 'bilingual' communication. More explicit teaching about signing to mainstream school children would probably have overcome this. It may also have helped to clarify the distinction between hearing impairments and cognitive disabilities.

Mainstream school children often needed more time to learn signs. Sometimes the sequence of signs introduced was arbitrary. Signs were learned to go with a particular story but were not used after that one session, whereas some signs such as 'toilet', 'sit', 'hello' and 'goodbye' were used again and again. With hindsight, it would have been useful to have identified a small core of key signs and taught these systematically to mainstream school children outside link sessions. Special school pupils tended to become bored in link sessions when mainstream school children were being taught signs. Alternatively the special school pupils may have been able to teach the signs. Despite these difficulties there were some interesting examples of mainstream school children, especially in the Link 7 project, using signs spontaneously, for example to reinforce a teacher's spoken instruction. These children were probably less inhibited than many adults would have been in trying to sign.

All classroom notices in the mainstream school involved in the Link 7 project were in traditional orthography; use could have been made of Makaton symbols in some of these notices. The special school in which Link 11 sessions took place did use Makaton symbols in classroom notices but these were rarely drawn to the attention of mainstream school children. These types of change would have made the classrooms more genuinely 'bilingual' and so encouraged the use and acceptability of both 'languages'. Oliver Sachs (1989) has argued that sign language is an important part of the culture of the deaf. Arguably, signing systems for people with learning difficulties are similarly part of their culture, not just a form of communication to be treated as secondary to spoken language. The latter attitude isolates those who use sign language when they are in environments in which it is not used. Teachers and pupils in inclusive schools need to be prepared to learn and to use relevant sign systems with pupils for whom these are a major means of communciation.

RESPECT FOR INDIVIDUALS

Several earlier points relate to fostering respect for individuals. This also raises difficult areas as respecting an individual's position may conflict with other goals. Pupils involved in link schemes may have apprehensions about specific aspects of that involvement. For example, in a link project not described in this book a 10 year old from a mainstream school worked happily with pupils with severe learning difficulties but was frightened by pupils at the same special school who had profound and multiple learning difficulties. As a result, he began to stay away from school when link project activities were taking place. One may argue that it was not the child but the school ethos, the link approach, or preparation for the work which was at fault. However, as moves towards inclusion, or integration, do not take place in a perfect world these sorts of fears do occur and need to be recognised. Encouraging children (from special and mainstream schools) to talk openly about such feelings should reveal these apprehensions and so help teachers and parents to deal with them.

It is also important that within the type of project described here, pupils have a choice of work partner so that no child, whether from a special or mainstream school, is pushed into working with someone with whom he or she feels uncomfortable. Importantly, in both the link projects described here special and mainstream school pupils took it in turns to choose work partners from the other school group. Partners were not allocated by adults nor were mainstream school children always making the choices.

The importance of feeling good about oneself, an intended outcome of an ethos that reflects respect for individuals, was reflected strongly in the views of the pupils at schools for pupils with moderate learning difficulties. Many of their best memories of mainstream schools concerned occasions on which they had been made to feel positively special.

ADULTS' RESPONSES TO 'MISBEHAVIOUR'

A recurrent topic in interview responses by children from the school for pupils with moderate learning difficulties (see Chapter 2) and from mainstream school children in both link projects concerned how adults responded to pupils' misbehaviour. This arose, in particular, in the Link 7 project in which many of the mainstream school children were concerned about what they saw as the 'naughtiness' of some special school children. To some extent these children may have been reflecting staff concerns. Some staff (special and mainstream school) said that they were unsure about disciplining pupils from the other school. The concern was reflected in the diary of one of the mainstream school teachers. After the first session she wrote, 'I must realise that I can never turn my back with these [special school] children.' After a later session she recorded concerns about two children from the special school running, covered in paint, into a neighbouring classroom and feelings that this reflected badly on the order (or perceived lack of it) in the link project classroom. Whose role was discipline in a classroom in which staff from both schools were working? Was it to be assumed that all pupils were subject to the same rules?

In link projects such questions highlight the need for communication between the adults involved, clear and explicitly agreed codes of behaviour for all pupils and any (probably rare) exceptions to these for individual children. A problem may be finding time for this communication and there are no easy answers to this, but it is an issue beyond integration/inclusion. Teachers in these projects often made arrangements by telephone because face to face meetings were not possible to fit into the (already overcrowded) timetables. One authority created integration support teacher posts, based in special schools, to allow non-contact time between teachers. The work of the integration support teachers has been described more fully by Barry Carpenter and his colleagues (see Carpenter et al., 1988; Carpenter and Lewis, 1988).

Staff involved in the link projects discussed here came to the conclusion that all pupils in the classroom were subject to the same rules and that these should be enforced. It was felt that it was not a good policy to 'let off' special school pupils for behaviour which would not have been condoned in mainstream school pupils. Establishing, in principle, a common rule leaves the adults with the task of how to convey that rule to pupils. Some special school staff involved in the Link 7 project were apprehensive that their reprimands to special school pupils may have appeared overharsh to mainstream school pupils. A teacher from one of the special schools noted in the diary of the project:

I had to tell Michelle [mainstream school girl] 'You have to be firm [with special school children]'. Most of the mainstream school children are hesitant about telling our children off.

Schools may be divided about this issue. On the one hand, treating all pupils similarly in terms of discipline may be regarded as the best policy because it does not create double standards. On the other hand, it may be seen as negating different individual needs. Whatever the decision, the important points are the need for open discussion about this between staff and an agreed policy.

Discussion with pupils about the nature of, and responses to, behavioural difficulties is likely to be useful in helping pupils to understand appropriate expectations. In addition, adults' interactions with children are likely to be important role models for classmates. Val Roberts and Sue Dudek have written of a 6 year old with severe emotional problems who was integrated successfully into a mainstream school:

> When Mark arrived he was aggressive towards adults, unco-operative and attention seeking . . . He jeered and mimicked his teacher, threw books and pencils around the classroom, pushed chairs and furniture, stood on tables and shouted abuse. The first time this happened, all in a ten minute session, he was withdrawn from the classroom . . . While he was out of the classroom, his teacher took the opportunity to discuss Mark's behaviour with her shocked and silent class. They were told that he was very unhappy and found difficulty in doing certain things. They were asked to ignore his behaviour and to help him whenever possible . . . . Mark is [now] accepted by all the children and plays quite happily.
>
> (1985: 32–3)

Val Roberts and Sue Dudek also emphasise the support of all the staff, the involvement of an education welfare officer and help provided by an educational psychologist as central to Mark's successful integration.

THE IMPORTANCE OF MONITORING INTEGRATION AND INCLUSION

The link projects were planned and carried out by staff from the schools involved. My role was in working with those staff to monitor whether goals were being met through the projects. This close monitoring revealed that some anticipated outcomes did materialise (for example, there was a general tolerance and ability of diverse pupils to work productively together). In general, pairs worked better than threesomes of one special and two mainstream school pupils. (It is interesting to compare this with the similar finding of Bennett and Cass, 1988, who investigated interactions in threesomes of relatively high and/or low attaining children.) Similarly, there was more interaction between special and mainstream school pupils in small groups (less than three) than in larger groups (up to eight).

Some outcomes were unexpected, such as the extent to which the link projects seemed to draw out pupils' communication skills, and the confusion in understanding about disability by even the older (10- and 11-year-old) mainstream school pupils. A particularly unexpected finding for the adults was that adult involvement often impeded rather than enhanced pupils' interactions. The point was noted explicitly by one special school teacher, 'Interactions did emerge between special and mainstream school pupils – usually when the adults took a back seat.' Pupils were inclined to defer to adults if they were close at hand, rather than to interact with one another. Teachers and other adults present concluded that the most useful role for them, having established a clear task and supportive structure, was of a detached but vigilant observer.

It is vital that adults and the parents of children involved in link schemes and related work have the time, motivation and energy to stand back from their immediate involvement to reflect on the aims and whether these are being met. For example, some adults involved may become concerned about the quality of an end product, such as a collage or model. However, this is relatively unimportant if the aims are purely social; if the aims are cognitive, as well as social, then progress towards both these aims needs to be assessed as reliably as possible.

Both the predicted and the unexpected outcomes of these link projects underline the importance of monitoring what is happening in such projects. Gordon Stobbart asks 'Can psychology justify the integration of special needs children?' and answers – yes, but only under certain conditions. He concludes, 'What has to be resisted is any approach which avoids questions about the *quality* of the [integration] arrangements being offered' (1992: 34). To date, there is a large bank of evidence and discussion from a range of countries about integration and inclusion in relation to political issues, finance, the curriculum, observational overviews, parental and teachers' views. These are important but they provide only part of the picture. Direct evidence about the fine-grained detail of the views and interactions of the children involved is vital.

The last words go to a 36-year-old man with Down's syndrome (Jahoda *et al.*, 1988). His wishes match those of the teachers involved in the link projects. The evidence about interactions in these projects and the views of children in segregated special school provision point to the conclusion that carefully monitored inclusion is a feasible, reasonable and mutually beneficial goal:

> People should realise that we are people like them and want to be treated like them, so that you are in the same standards. But not saying 'Well I want to be your friend because you're handicapped'. To me that's wrong, totally, generally. It would be much nicer to know people coming up to say 'I'm your friend and I want to know more about you as a person' not just that big word that doesn't mean anything.
>
> (1988: 113)

Suggestions for selected further reading

CHAPTER 1

The comparative dimension in integration

Barton, L. (ed.) (1989) *Integration: Myth or Reality?*, Lewes: Falmer.
Daunt, P. (1991) *Meeting Disability: A European response*, London: Cassell.
Kauffman, J.M. (1989) The Regular Education Initiative as Reagan–Bush education policy. A trickle-down theory of education to the hard-to-teach, *Journal of Special Education*, 23(3): 256–79.
Marchesi, A., Echelta, G., Martin, E., Bavio, M. and Galan, M. (1991) Assessment of the integration project in Spain, *European Journal of Special Needs Education*, 6(3): 185–200.
Meijer, C.J.W., Pijl, S.J. and Hegarty, S. (1994) *New Perspectives in Special Education: A six country study of integration*, London: Routledge.
Pijl, S.J. and Meijer, C.J.W. (1991) Does integration count for much? An analysis of the practices of integration in eight countries, *European Journal of Special Needs Education*, 6(2): 100–11.
Slee, R. (ed.) (1993) *Is There a Desk with My Name on it? The Politics of Integration*, Lewes: Falmer.
Walton, W.T., Emanuelsson, I. and Rosenqvist, J. (1990) Normalisation and integration of handicapped students into the regular education system: contrasts between Sweden and the United States of America, *European Journal of Special Needs Education*, 5(2): 111–25.
Ward, J. (1993) Special education in Australia and New Zealand, pp. 130–42 in P. Mittler, R. Brouillette and D. Harris (eds) *Special Needs Education (World Yearbook of Education 1993)*, London: Kogan Page.

CHAPTER 2

Children's views of schooling

Ainley, J. and Bourke, S. (1992) Student views of primary schooling, *Research Papers in Education*, 7(2): 107–28.

Blatchford, P., Creeser, R. and Mooney, A. (1990) Playground games and playtime: The children's view, *Educational Research*, 32(3): 163–74.

Meighan, R. (1977) The pupil as client: The learner's experience of schooling, *Educational Review*, 29(2): 123–35.

Pollard, A. (1985) *The Social World of the Primary School*, London: Holt, Rinehart and Winston.

Woods, P. (1990) *The Happiest Days?*, Lewes: Falmer.

Interview methodology, with particular reference to interviewing people with learning difficulties

Breakwell, G. (1990) *Interviewing*, London: BPS/Leicester.

Doris, J. (ed.) (1991) *The suggestibility of children's recollections: Implications for eye witness testimony*, Washington, DC: American Psychological Associates.

Flynn, M.C. (1986) Adults who are mentally handicapped as consumers: Issues and guidelines, *Journal of Mental Deficiency Research*, 30: 369–77.

Lee, R.M. (1993) *Doing Research on Sensitive Topics*, London: Sage.

Pollard, A. (1987) Studying children's perspectives – a collaborative approach, pp. 95–118 in G. Walford (ed.) *Doing Sociology of Education*, Lewes: Falmer.

Powney, J. and Watts, M. (1987) *Interviewing in Educational Research*, London: Routledge.

Sigelman, C.K., Budd, E.C., Winer, J.L., Schoenrock, C.J. and Maryin, P.W. (1982) Evaluating alternative techniques of questioning mentally retarded persons, *American Journal of Mental Deficiency*, 86: 511–18.

Spencer, J.R. and Flin, R. (1990) *The Evidence of Children*, London: Blackstone Press.

Tomlinson, P. (1989) Having it both ways: Hierarchical focusing as research interview method, *British Educational Research Journal*, 15(2): 155–76.

CHAPTER 3

Bereavement and children

Glassock, G.T. and Rowling, L. (1992) *Learning to Grieve*, Newtown, Australia: Millenium Books.

Gordon, A. and Klass, D. (1979) *They Need to Know: How to Teach Children about Death*, New York: Prentice Hall.

Hughes, J. (1981) *Questions Children Ask*, London: Lion Publishing.

Lendrelle, S. and Syme, G. (1992) *Gift of Tears: A practical approach to loss and bereavement counselling*, London: Routledge.

Matthias, B. and Spiers, D. (1992) *A Handbook on Death and Bereavement: Helping Children Understand*, London: National Library for the Handicapped Child.

Reed, E.L. (1970) *Helping Children with the Mystery of Death*, Nashville, TN: Abingdon Press.

Ward, B, (1993) *Good Grief: Exploring Feelings, Loss and Death with Under Elevens*, London: Kingsley.

Wass, H. and Corr, C.A. (1982) *Helping Children Cope with Death*, New York: McGraw-Hill.

Wells, R. (1988) *Helping Children Cope with Grief*, London: Sheldon Press.

Wynnejones, P. (1985) *Children, Death and Bereavement*, London: Scripture Union.

Children's attitudes towards, and understanding of, disability

Byrnne, E.A., Cunningham, C.C. and Sloper, P. (1988) *Families and Their Children with Down's Syndrome: One Feature in Common*, London: Routledge.

Hazzard, A. (1983) Children's experience with, knowledge of, and attitudes toward disabled persons, *Journal of Special Education*, 17(2): 131–9.

Horne, M.D. (1985) *Attitudes toward Handicapped Students: Professional, Peer and Parent Relationships*, Hillsdale, NJ: Lawrence Erlbaum.

Quicke, J., Beasley, K. and Morrison, C. (1990) *Challenging Prejudice through Education*, Lewes: Falmer.

Sheldon, D. (1991) How was it for you? Pupils', parents' and teachers' perspectives on integration, *British Journal of Special Education*, 18(3): 107–10.

Soder, M. (1990) Prejudice or ambivalence? Attitudes towards persons with disabilities, *Disability, Handicap and Society*, 5(3): 227–41.

Thomas, D. (1982) *The Experience of Handicap*, London: Methuen.

Ward, J. and Center, Y. (1987) Attitudes to the integration of disabled children into regular classes: A factor analysis of functional characteristics, *British Journal of Educational Psychology*, 57(2): 221–4.

Yuker, H.E. (1988) *Attitudes Towards Persons with Disabilities*, New York: Springer.

Resources concerned with the promotion of positive attitudes towards disabled people

Bedford Video Group (1993) *Our Lives* (video), Nuneaton: Bedford Video Group

McConkey, R. and McCormack, B. (1983) *Breaking Barriers: Educating People about Disability*, London: Souvenir.

O'Brien, J. and Forest, M. with Snow, J., Pearpoint, J. and Hasbury, D. (1989) *Action for Inclusion*, Toronto: Inclusion Press.

Pearpoint, J., Forest, M. and Snow, J. (1992) *Strategies to Make Inclusion Work*, Toronto: Inclusion Press.

Rieser, R. and Mason, M. (1990) *Disability Equality in the Classroom*, London: ILEA (Inner London Education Authority).

Understanding Disability Educational Trust (UDET) (1993) *Understanding Disability*, London: UDET.

See also

Barnicoats (1992) *Special Needs Catalogue*, Penryn: Barnicoats.
Mathias, B. (1991) *Special Needs: A Penguin Booklist*, London: Penguin.
'One World' series, published by Franklin Watts, London. This series includes *I have Down's Syndrome* by B. Pettenuzzo (1987) and similar titles focusing on specific conditions and disabilities.

CHAPTERS 4 AND 5

Children's peer tutoring and cooperative working in classrooms

Allen, V.L. (1976) *Children as Teachers*, New York: Academic Press.
Biott, C. and Easen, P. (1994) *Collaborative Learning in Staffrooms and Classrooms*, London: David Fulton.
Cohen, P.A., Kulik, J.A. and Kulik, C.L.C. (1982) Educational outcomes of tutoring: A meta-analysis of findings, *American Educational Research Journal*, 19(2): 237–48.
Cooper, C.C., Ayers-Lopez, S. and Marquis, A. (1982) Children's discourse during peer learning in experimental and naturalistic situations, *Discourse Processes*, 5: 177–91.
Dunne, E. and Bennett, N. (1990) *Talking and Learning in Groups*, London: Macmillan.
Foot, H.C., Morgan, M.J. and Shute, R.H. (eds) (1990) *Children Helping Children*, Chichester: Wiley.
Glynn, T. (1985) Contexts for independent learning, *Educational Psychology*, 5(1): 5–15.
Goodlad, S. and Hirst, B. (eds) (1990) *Explorations in Peer Tutoring*, Oxford: Blackwell.
Johnson, D.W. and Johnson, R.T. (1987) *Learning Together and Alone* (2nd edition), London: Prentice Hall International.
Rogoff, B. (1990) *Apprenticeship in Thinking*, Oxford: Oxford University Press.
Slavin, R.E. (ed.) (1985) *Learning to Cooperate, Cooperating to Learn*, New York: Plenum.
Topping, K. (1988) *The Peer Tutoring Handbook*, London: Croom Helm.
Webb, N.M. (1989) Peer interaction and learning in small groups, *International Journal of Educational Research*, 13(1): 21–40.

Language development

Buckley, S. and Bird, G. (1993) *The development of language and reading skills in children with Down's syndrome*, Portsmouth: Sarah Duffen Centre, University of Portsmouth.

Clarke, A.D.B. and Clarke, A.M. (eds) (1985) *Mental Deficiency: The Changing Outlook (Remediation)*, London: Methuen.

Durkin, K. (ed.) (1986) *Language Development in the School Years*, London: Croom Helm.

Fletcher, P. and Garman, M. (eds) (1986) *Language Acquisition*, Cambridge: Cambridge University Press.

Garvey, C. (1984) *Children's Talk*, London: Fontana.

Goldbart, J. (1986) The development of language and communication, pp. 153–82 in J. Coupe and J. Porter (eds) *The Education of Children with Severe Learning Difficulties*, London: Croom Helm.

Lloyd, P. (1982) Talking to some purpose, pp. 196–215 in M. Beveridge (ed.) *Children Thinking Through Language*, London: Arnold.

Oakhill, J. and Garnham, A. (1988) *Becoming a Skilled Reader*, Oxford: Blackwell.

Robinson, W.P. (ed.) (1981) *Communication in Development*, New York: Academic Press.

Romaine, S. (1984) *The Language of Children and Adolescents*, Oxford: Blackwell.

Schiefelbusch, R.L. and Pickar, J. (eds) (1984) *The Acquisition of Communicative Competence*, Baltimore, MD: University Park Press.

Smith, P.K. and Cowie, H. (1991) *Understanding Children's Development*, Oxford: Blackwell.

Tann, S. (1991) *Developing Language in the Primary Classroom*, London: Cassell.

Wells, G. (1986) *The Meaning Makers*, London: Heinemann.

References

Aboud, F. (1988) *Children and Prejudice*, Oxford: Blackwell.

Ackerman, D. and Mount, H. (1991) *Literacy for All*, London: David Fulton.

Ainscow, M. with Kerr, T and Norwich, B. (1993) *Towards Effective Schools for All*, Stafford: National Association for Special Educational Needs (NASEN).

Anderson, R. (1989) *The Bus People*, Oxford: Oxford University Press.

Armstrong, D., Galloway, D. and Tomlinson, S. (1993) Assessing special educational needs: The child's contribution, *British Educational Research Journal*, 19(2): 121–32.

Ashman, A.F. and Conway, R.N.F. (1989) *Cognitive Strategies for Special Education*, London: Routledge.

Astington, J.W., Harris, P.L. and Olson, D.R. (eds) (1988) *Developing Theories of Mind*, Oxford: Blackwell.

Atkinson, D. and Williams, F. (1990) *Know Me As I Am*, London: Hodder and Stoughton.

Audit Commission/HMI (Her Majesty's Inspectorate) (1992) *Getting in on the Act*, London: HMSO.

Bell, G.H. and Colbeck, B. (1989) *Experiencing Integration*, London: Falmer.

Bennett, N. and Cass, A. (1988) The effects of group composition on group interactive processes and pupil understanding, *British Educational Research Journal*, 15(1): 19–32.

Bennett, N. and Cass, A. (1989) *From Special to Ordinary Schools: Case Studies in Integration*, London: Cassell.

Beresford, E. (1981) *The Four of Us*, London: Hutchinson.

Beveridge, S. (1993) *Special Educational Needs in Schools*, London: Routledge.

Booth, T. and Potts, P. (1983) *Integrating Special Education*, Oxford: Blackwell.

Bryan, T. (1986) A review of studies on learning disabled children's communicative competence, pp. 227–59 in R.L. Schiefelbusch (ed.) - *Language Competence: Assessment and Intervention*, London: Taylor and Francis.

Bryan, T., Donahue, M. and Pearl, R. (1981) Learning disabled children's peer interactions during a small group problem solving task, *Learning Disability Quarterly*, 4: 13–22.

Bryan, T., Wheeler, R., Felcan, J. and Henek, T. (1976) 'Come on Dummy': An observational study of children's communications, *Journal of Learning Disabilities*, 9: 53–61.

Budoff, M. and Siperstein, G.N. (1978) Low income children's attitudes towards mentally handicapped children: Effects of labelling and academic behaviour, *American Journal of Mental Deficiency*, 82(5): 474–9.

Carpenter, B. and Lewis, A. (1988) Searching for solutions: Approaches to planning the curriculum for integration of SLD and PMLD children, pp. 103–24 in D. Baker and K. Bovair (eds) *Making the Ordinary School Special?*, Lewes: Falmer.

Carpenter, B., Lewis, A. and Moore, J. (1987) An integration project, *New South Wales Journal of Special Education*, 1(1): 20–4.

Carpenter, B., Fathers, J., Lewis, A. and Privett, R. (1988) Integration: The Coleshill experience, *British Journal of Special Education*, 15(3): 119–21.

Cohen, E.G. (1994) Restructuring the classroom: Conditions for productive small groups, *Review of Educational Research*, 64(1): 1–36.

Cole, A. (1993) Scratch the surface of public tolerance, *The Guardian*, 25 August.

Conti-Ramsden, G. and Taylor, J. (1990) Teacher–pupil talk: Integrated vs segregated environments for children with severe learning difficulties, *British Journal of Disorders of Communication*, 25: 1–15.

Cooper, P. (1993) *Effective Schools for Disaffected Students*, London: Routledge.

Coopers and Lybrand (1992) *Within Reach: Access for disabled children to mainstream education*, London: Spastics Society/NUT.

Copeland, J. and Hodges, J. (1976) *For the Love of Ann*, London: Arrow.

Corbett, J. (1991) So, who wants to be normal?, *Disability, Handicap and Society*, 6(3): 259–60.

Corbett, J., Jones, E. and Ralph, S. (1993) A shared presentation: Two disabled women on video, *Disability, Handicap and Society*, 8(2): 173–86.

Crocker, A.C. and Cheeseman, R.G. (1988) The ability of young children to rank themselves for ability, *Educational Studies*, 14(1): 105–10.

Croll, P. and Moses, D. (1985) *One in Five*, London: Routledge and Kegan Paul.

Cullingford, C. (1991) *The Inner World of the School*, London: Cassell.

Davies, B. (1982) *Life in the Classroom and Playground: the accounts of primary school children*, London: Routledge and Kegan Paul.

Department of Education and Science (DES) (1978) *Special Educational Needs* (The Warnock Report), London: HMSO.

Department of Education and Science (DES) (1992) *Statistics of Education: Schools 1991*, London: DES.

Department of Health (1993) *Mental Illness: What does it mean?*, London: Department of Health.

Detheridge, T. (1993) Symbolic significance, *Times Educational Supplement*, 5 November, p. 30.

Donahue, M. (1983) Learning-disabled children as conversational partners, *Topics in Language Disorders*, 4: 15–27.

Dore, J. (1986) The development of conversational competence, pp. 3–60 in R.L. Schiefelbusch (ed.) *Language Competence, Assessment and Intervention*, London: Taylor and Francis.

Duffin, S. (1981) quoted in M.D. Orlansky and W.L. Heward (eds) *Voices: Interviews with Handicapped People*, p. viii, Columbus, OH: Merrill.

Dunne, E. and Bennett, N. (1990) *Talking and Learning in Groups*, London: Macmillan.

Fairbairn, G. and Fairbairn, S. (eds) (1992) *Integrating Special Children: Some ethical issues*, Aldershot: Avebury.

Fathers, J. (1994) Personal communication.

Fletcher-Campbell, F. (1994) *Still Joining Forces?*, Slough: NFER (National Foundation for Educational Research, UK).

Forehand, R.L. and McMahon, R.J. (1981) *Helping the Non-Compliant Child*, New York: Guiford Press.

Forest, M. and Pearpoint, J. (1992) Two roads: Inclusion or exclusion, pp. 8–12 in J. Pearpoint, M. Forest and J. Snow (eds) *The Inclusion Papers: Strategies to make inclusion work*, Toronto: Inclusion Press.

Frankenberg, W.K. (1981) *Denver Developmental Reference Chart*, University of Colorado, Denver, Colorado.

Franklin, B.M. (ed.) (1987) *Learning Disability: Dissenting Essays*, Lewes: Falmer.

Fuchs, D. and Fuchs, L.S. (1994) Inclusive schools movement and the radicalisation of special education reform, *Exceptional Children*, 60(4): 294–309.

Fuchs, L.S., Fuchs, D., Bentz, J., Phillips, N.B. and Hamlett, C.L. (1994) The nature of student interactions during peer tutoring with and without prior training and experience, *American Educational Research Journal*, 31(1): 75–103.

Fulcher, G. (1989) *Disabling Policies? A comparative approach to education policy and disability*, Lewes: Falmer.

Gallagher, T.M. and Darnton, B. (1978) Conversational aspects of the speech of language disordered children: Revision behaviors, *Journal of Speech and Hearing Research*, 21: 118–35.

Galloway, F. (1989) *Personal and Social Education in the Primary School*, Exeter: Pergamon.

Garvey, C. (1984) *Children's Talk*, London: Fontana.

Gillham, B. (1981) *My Brother Barry*, London: Andre Deutsch.

Glassock, G.T. and Rowling, L. (1992) *Learning to Grieve*, Newtown, Australia: Millenium Books.

Gross, J. (1993) *Special Educational Needs in the Primary School*, Milton Keynes: Open University Press.

Grossman, H. (ed.) (1983) *Manual on Terminology and Classification in Mental Retardation*, Washington, DC: American Association on Mental Deficiency.

Guralnick, M.J. (1990) Peer interactions and the development of handicapped children's social and communicative competence, pp. 275–306 in H.C. Foot, M.J. Morgan and R.H. Shute (eds) *Children Helping Children*, London: Wiley.

Guralnick, M.J. and Paul-Brown, D. (1980) Functional and discourse analyses of non-handicapped pre-school children's speech to handi-capped children, *American Journal of Mental Deficiency*, 84(5): 444–54.

Guralnick, M.J. and Paul-Brown, D. (1984) Communicative adjustments during behaviour–request episodes among children at different devel-opmental levels, *Child Development*, 55: 911–19.

Guralnick, M.J. and Paul-Brown, D. (1989) Peer-related communicative competence of pre-school children: Developmental and adaptive char-acteristics, *Journal of Speech and Hearing Research*, 32: 930–43.

Hall, J. (1992) Segregation by another name?, *Special Children*, 56: 20–3.

Hardie, S., with Hardie, H. and Hardie, A. (1991) *Why me? 'Autobiography' of Sheenagh Hardy*, London: Excaliber Press.

Heath, R. and Levin, P. (1991) Cultural sensitivity in the design and evaluation of early intervention programmes, pp. 67–92 in D. Mitchell and R.I. Brown (eds) *Early Intervention Studies for Young Children with Special Needs*, London: Chapman and Hall.

Hebden, J. (1985) *She'll Never Do Anything, Dear*, London: Souvenir Press.

Hegarty, S. (1993) Conclusion, p. 30 in M. Ainscow, with T. Kerr and B. Norwich *Towards Effective Schools for All*, Stafford: NASEN (National Association for Special Educational Needs).

Hegarty, S. and Pocklington, K. with Lucas, D. (1981) *Educating Pupils with Special Needs in the Ordinary School*, Windsor: NFER/Nelson.

Hegarty, S. and Pocklington, K. with Lucas, D. (1982) *Integration in Action*, Windsor: NFER/Nelson.

Henderson, R.A. (1993) What is this 'Least Restrictive Environment' in the United States?, pp. 93–106 in R. Slee (ed.) *Is There a Desk with My Name on it?*, Lewes: Falmer.

Herbert, E. and Carpenter, B. (1994) Fathers: the secondary partners, *Children and Society*, 8(1): 31–41.

Hewstone, M. and Brown, R. (1986) *Contact and Conflict in Intergroup Encounters*, Oxford: Blackwell.

Hornby, G. (1991) Parental involvement, pp. 206–24 in D. Mitchell and R.I. Brown (eds) *Early Intervention Studies for Young Children with Special Needs*, London: Chapman and Hall.

Hornby, G. (1992) Integration of children with special needs – is it time for a policy review?, *Support for Learning*, 7(3): 130–4.

Hull, J.M. (1990) *Touching the Rock*, London: SPCK.

Hunt, M. (1994) Planning and Diversity: Special schools and their alterna-tives, Paper to Policy Options in Special Needs Seminar, NASEN (National Association for Special Educational Needs), University of London, Institute of Education, March 1994.

Hutt, E. (1986) *Teaching Language Disordered Children*, London: Arnold.

Jahoda, A., Markova, I. and Cattermole, M. (1988) Stigma and the self-concept of people with a mental handicap, *Journal of Mental Deficiency Research*, 32: 103–15.

Jenkinson, J.C. (1993) Integration of students with severe and multiple learning difficulties, *European Journal of Special Needs Education*, 8(3): 320–35.

Jennings, S. (1993) *Art Therapy and Dramatherapy: Masks of the Soul*, London: Jessica Kingsley.

Jennings, S. (1994) *Dramatherapy and Learning Difficulties*, London: Jessica Kingsley.

Jordan, R.R. and Powell, S.D. (1994) Whose curriculum? Critical notes on integration and entitlement, *European Journal of Special Needs Education*, 9(1): 27–39.

Jowett, S., Hegarty, S. and Moses, D. (1988) *Joining Forces*, Windsor: NFER/Nelson.

Kidd, R. and Hornby, G. (1993) Transfer from special to mainstream, *British Journal of Special Education*, 20(1): 17–19.

Kirk, S.A., Gallagher, J.J. and Anastasiow, N.J. (1993) *Educating Exceptional Children*, Boston: Houghton Mifflin.

Kyle, C. and Davies, K. (1991) Attitudes of mainstream pupils towards mental retardation, *British Journal of Special Education*, 18(3): 103–6.

Lang, P. (1988) *Thinking about . . . Personal and Social Education in the Primary School*, Oxford: Blackwell.

Larsen, H. (1974) *Don't Forget Tom*, London: A. and C. Black.

Leicester, M. (1992) Integrating inequality: Prejudice, power and special needs, pp. 79–91 in G. Fairbairn and S. Fairbairn (eds) *Integrating Special Children: Some ethical issues*, Avebury: Ashgate.

Leslie, A.M. (1987) Pretense and representation: The origins of 'theory of mind', *Psychological Review*, 94: 412–26.

Lewis, A. (1990) Six and seven year old 'normal' children's talk to peers with severe learning difficulties, *European Journal of Special Needs Education*, 5(1): 13–23.

Lewis, A. (1991) *Primary Special Needs and the National Curriculum*, London: Routledge.

Lewis, A. (1992) Group child interviews as a research tool, *British Educational Research Journal*, 18(4): 413–22.

Lewis, A. (1993a) Integration, education and rights, *British Educational Research Journal*, 19(3): 285–96.

Lewis, A. (1993b) Primary school children's understanding of severe learning difficulties, *Educational Psychology*, 13(2): 133–46.

Lewis, A. (1995) Views of schooling held by children attending schools for pupils with moderate learning difficulties (MLD/MID), *International Journal of Disability, Development and Education*, 42.

Lewis, A. and Carpenter, B. (1990) Discourse, in an integrated school setting, between six and seven year old non-handicapped children and peers with severe learning difficulties, pp. 270–8 in W.I. Fraser (ed.) *Key Issues in Mental Retardation*, London: Routledge.

Lewis, A. and Lewis, V. (1987) The attitudes of young children towards peers with severe learning difficulties, *British Journal of Developmental Psychology*, 5(3): 287–92.

Lewis, A. and Lewis, V. (1988) Young children's attitudes, after a period of integration, towards peers with severe learning difficulties, *European Journal of Special Needs Education*, 3(3): 161–72.

Lewis, J. (1993) Integration in Victoria schools: Radical social policy or old wine?, pp. 9–26 in R. Slee (ed.) *Is There a Desk with My Name on it?*, Lewes: Falmer.

Light, P. (1987) Taking roles, pp. 41–61 in J. Bruner and H. Haste (eds) *Making Sense*, London: Methuen.

Livesley, W.J. and Bromley, D.B. (1973) *Person Perception in Childhood and Adolescence*, London: Wiley.

Lloyd, P. (1982) Talking to some purpose, pp. 196–215 in M. Beveridge (ed.) *Children Thinking Through Language*, London: Arnold.

Locke, A. (1985) *Living Language*, Windsor: NFER/Nelson.

Maas, E., Maracek, E. and Travers, J.R. (1978) Children's conceptions of disordered behaviour, *Child Development*, 49: 146–54.

McConkey, R. and McCormack, B. (1984) Changing attitudes to people who are disabled, *Mental Handicap*, 12: 112–14.

McCormack, M. (1992) *Special Children, Special Needs*, London: Thorsons.

McTear, M.F. and Conti-Ramsden, G. (1992) *Pragmatic Disability in Children*, London: Whurr Publishers.

Maras, P. (1993) The integration of children with disabilities into the mainstream: Effects of school and age on children's attitudes toward disability, Unpublished PhD Thesis, University of Kent at Canterbury.

Maras, P. and Brown, R. (1992) 'I don't know if children in wheelchairs can hear': Mainstream children's attitudes to disability, *British Psychological Society, Division of Educational & Child Psychology Newsletter*, 4: 30–5, also in *Education Section Review*, 16(2): 72–7.

Martlew, M. and Hodson, J. (1991) Children with mild learning difficulties in an integrated and in a special class, *British Journal of Educational Psychology*, 61(3): 355–72.

Mason, H. and Mudd, S. (1993) *Speaking and Listening Activities*, Bright Ideas for Early Years Series, Leamington: Scholastic.

Mason, M. (1990) in R. Rieser and M. Mason *Disability Equality in the Classroom*, London: ILEA.

Meijer, C.J.W., Pijl, S.J. and Hegarty, S. (1994) *New Perspectives in Special Education: A six country study of integration*, London: Routledge.

Mittler, P. (1990) Prospects for disabled children and their families: An international perspective, *Disability, Handicap and Society*, 51: 53–64.

Mittler, P. (1992) Whose needs? Whose interests?, pp. 105–20 in G. Fairbairn and S. Fairbairn (eds) *Integrating Special Children: Some ethical issues*, Aldershot: Avebury.

Mooney, A., Creeser, R. and Blatchford, P. (1991) Children's views on teasing and fighting in junior schools, *Educational Research*, 33(2): 103–12.

MORI (Market and Opinion Research International) (1982) *Public Attitudes Towards the Mentally Handicapped*, London: MENCAP.

Mortimore, P., Sammons, P., Stoll, L., Lewis, D. and Ecob, R. (1988) *School Matters*, London: Open Books.

Mosley, J. (1991) *All Round Success*, Trowbridge: Wiltshire County Council.

Mosley, J. (1993) *Turn Your School Round*, Wisbech: LDA.

Mosley, J. (1994) Developing self-esteem, *Special Children*, Back to Basics 12, no. 74, pp. 1–8 (inset).

Mousley, J.A., Rice, M. and Tregenza, K. (1993) Integration of students with disabilities into regular schools: Policy in use, *Disability, Handicap and Society*, 8(1): 59–70.

Mueller, E. (1972) The maintenance of verbal exchanges between young children, *Child Development*, 43: 930–8.

Nabuzoka, D., Whitney, I., Smith, P.K. and Thompson, D. (1993) Bullying and children with special educational needs, pp. 189–200 in D. Tattum (ed.) *Understanding and Managing Bullying*, London: Heinemann.

Norman, K. (ed.) (1992) *Thinking Voices*, Sevenoaks: Hodder and Stoughton.

Norwich, B. (1990) *Reappraising Special Needs Education*, London: Cassell.

O'Brien, J. and Forest, M. with Snow, J., Pearpoint, J. and Hasbury, D. (1989) *Action for Inclusion*, Toronto: Inclusion Press.

O'Hanlon, C. (1993) *Special Education Integration in Europe*, London: David Fulton.

OMEP (1991) *Children with Special Needs in Mainstream Education*, London: OMEP.

Orlansky, M.D. and Heward, W.L. (1981) *Voices: Interviews with Handicapped People*, Columbus, OH: Merrill.

Pearpoint, J., Forest, M. and Snow, J. (1992) *Strategies to Make Inclusion Work*, Toronto: Inclusion Press.

Perner, J. (1991) *Understanding the Representational Mind*, Cambridge, MA: MIT Press.

Pollard, A., Broadfoot, P., Croll, P., Osborn, M. and Abbott, D. (1994) *Changing English Primary Schools: The Impact of the Education Reform Act*, London: Cassell.

Quicke, J., Beasley, K. and Morrison, C. (1990) *Challenging Prejudice through Education*, Lewes: Falmer.

Raban, B. and Lewis, A. (1994) Children with literacy difficulties, in D. Wray and J. Medwell (eds) *Teaching Primary English: The state of the art*, London: Routledge.

Ramasut, A. and Reynolds, D. (1993) Developing whole school approaches to special educational needs: From school effectiveness theory to school development practice, pp. 219–40 in R. Slee (ed.) *Is There a Desk with My Name on it?*, Lewes: Falmer.

Reuth, R. G., translated by K. Winston (1993) *The Life of Joseph Goebbels: The Mephistophelean Genius of Nazi Propaganda*, London: Constable.

Richardson, A. and Ritchie, J. (1989) *Developing Friendships*, London: Policy Studies Institute.

Rieser, R. and Mason, M. (1990) *Disability Equality in the Classroom*, London: ILEA (Inner London Education Authority).

Rispens, J. (1994) Rethinking the course of integration: What can we learn from the past?, pp. 132–40 in C.J. Meijer, S.J. Pijl and S. Hegarty (eds) *New Perspectives in Special Education: A six country study of integration*, London: Routledge.

Roaf, C. and Bines, H. (eds) (1989) *Needs, Rights and Opportunities*, London: Falmer.

Roberts, V. and Dudek, S. (1985) Integration and the first school, *Education 3–13*, 13(1): 31–3.

Robinson, E.J. and Robinson, W.P. (1986) Learning about verbal referential communication in the early school years, pp. 155–71 in K. Durkin (ed.) *Language Development in the School Years*, London: Croom Helm.

Rogoff, B. (1990) *Apprenticeship in Thinking*, Oxford: Oxford University Press.

Russell, P. (1991) Access to the National Curriculum for Parents, pp. 193–208 in R. Ashdown, B. Carpenter and K. Bovair (eds) *The Curriculum Challenge*, Lewes: Falmer.

Sachs, O. (1989) *Seeing Voices*, London: Pan.

Schiefelbusch, R.L. and Pickar, J. (eds) (1984) *The Acquisition of Communicative Competence*, Baltimore, MD: University Park Press.

Shatz, M. and Gelman, R. (1973) The development of communication skills: Modification in the speech of young children as a function of the listener, *Monograph of the Society for Research in Child Development*, 38(5): 1–36.

Shennan, V. (1980) *Ben*, London: Bodley Head.

Sheridan, M. (1973) *Children's Developmental Progress*, Windsor: NFER.

Shyer, M.F. (1980) *Welcome Home, Jellybean*, London: Macmillan.

Slee, R. (ed.) (1993) *Is There a Desk with My Name on it? The Politics of Integration*, Lewes: Falmer.

Stainback, S. and Stainback, W. (1992) *Curriculum Considerations in Inclusive Schooling*, Baltimore, MD: Paul Brookes.

Stainback, W. and Stainback, S. (1990) *Support Networks for Inclusive Schooling*, Baltimore, MD: Paul Brookes.

Stobbart, G. (1992) Can psychology justify the integration of children with special educational needs?, pp. 26–36 in G. Fairbairn and S. Fairbairn (eds) *Integrating Special Children: Some ethical issues*, Aldershot: Avebury.

Szivos, S. (1992) The limits to integration, pp. 112–33 in H. Brown and H. Smith (eds) *Normalisation: A Reader for the Nineties*, London: Routledge.

Tattum, D. and Tattum, E. (1992) *Social Education and Personal Development*, London: David Fulton.

Thomas, D. (1978) *The Social Psychology of Childhood Disability*, London: Methuen.

Thomas, M. quoted in D. Atkinson and F. Williams (eds) (1990) *Know Me as I am*, London: Hodder and Stoughton.

Thomson, A. (1993) Communicative competence in 5–8 year olds with mild or moderate learning difficulties and their classroom peers: referential and negotiation skills, *Social Development*, 2(3): 260–78.

Tilstone, C. (1992a) Severe learning difficulties, pp. 61–76 in R. Gulliford and G. Upton (eds) *Special Educational Needs*, London: Routledge.

Tilstone, C. (1992b) Pupils' views, pp. 32–9 in Tilstone, C. (ed.) *Teaching children with severe learning difficulties: practical applications*, London: David Fulton.

Tizard, B., Blatchford, P., Burke, J., Farquhar, C. and Plewis, I. (1988) *Young Children at School in the Inner City*, Hove: Lawrence Erlbaum Associates.

Uditsky, B. (1993) From integration to inclusion: The Canadian experience, pp. 79–92 in R. Slee (ed.) *Is There a Desk with my Name on it?*, Lewes: Falmer.

United Nations (1992) *United Nations Convention on the Rights of the Child*, extracts reprinted by the Children's Rights Development Unit (CRDU), London.

Wade, B. and Moore, M. (1992) *Experiencing Special Education*, Milton Keynes: Open University Press.

Waller, R. (1981) cited in M.D. Orlanski and W.L. Heward *Voices: Interviews with Handicapped People*, Columbus, OH: Merrill.

Wang, M.C., Reynolds, M.C. and Walberg, H.J. (eds) (1990) *Special Education: Research and Practice*, Oxford: Pergamon.

Ward, J., Center, Y. and Bochner, S. (1994) A question of attitudes: Integrating children with disabilities into regular classrooms?, *British Journal of Special Education*, 21(1): 34–9.

Weir, S. (1981) Our image of the disabled and how ready we are to help, *New Society*, 1 January, pp. 7–9.

Williams, D. (1992) *Nobody, Nowhere*, London: Transworld.

Williams, P. (1978) Our Mutual Handicap: Attitudes and perceptions of others by mentally handicapped people, Paper given to the International Cerebral Palsy Society, University College, Oxford, England, April.

Wolfendale, S. (1992) *Empowering Parents and Teachers: Working for Children*, London: Cassell.

Wolfendale, S. and Bryans, T. (1986) *Word Play: Language Activities for Young Children and their Parents*, Stafford: National Association for Special Educational Needs (NASEN).

Wood, D. (1993) On becoming a tutor: Towards an ontogenetic model, Paper presented at the ESRC InTER seminar 'Collaborative learning: What can children learn together, specific skills or general concepts?', Oxford, England, February.

Wood, S. (1988) Parents: Whose partners?, pp. 190–207 in L. Barton (ed.) *The Politics of Special Educational Needs*, Lewes: Falmer.

Yura, M.T. (1987) Family sub-system functions and disabled children: Some conceptual issues, pp. 135–51 in M. Ferrari and M.B. Sussman (eds) *Childhood Disability and Family Systems*, New York: Howarth.

Name index

Subject index